I0406877

A
CRY IN THE
WILDERNESS

The Raw
Confessions of
TEXAS SEVEN'S
JOSEPH GARCIA

JOSEPH GARCIA

With Selma Kerren

The opinions expressed in this manuscript are solely the opinions of
the author and do not represent the opinions or thoughts of the publisher.

A Cry In The Wilderness
The Raw Confessions of Texas Seven's Joseph Garcia All Rights Reserved
Copyright © 2007 Joseph Garcia
v 3.0

Cover Image © 2007 Jupiter Images Corporation
All Rights Reserved. Used With Permission.

Vienna Schilling Books

ISBN-10: 1466363665
ISBN-13: 9781466363663

Special thanks to:

Maria Martinez
Dallas, Texas
Because she ministers to
death row prisoners tirelessly
year after year.

Selma Kerren
Orange County, California
My co-writer on this book.

And Cathy Owen
Buckinghamshire, Great Britain
My Senior Editor
She got us ready for the world.

A Cry In The Wilderness
The Raw Confessions of Texas Seven's
Joseph Garcia

Kenedy, Texas, December 13, 2000.

Seven prisoners overpowered their guards and escaped from Connally Maximum Security Prison, s ixty-two miles southeast of San San Antonio, Texas.

Among them were Joseph Rivas, Larry Harper, Keith Newbury, Patrick Murphy, Joseph Garcia, Michael Rodriguez and young Randy Halprin, tagged by the media as The Texas Seven.

A van waited for them nearby and their cross-country flight began. Eleven days later on Christmas Eve, The Texas Seven robbed an Oshman's Sporting Goods Store at gunpoint in Irving, Texas, whereupon they shot and killed Police Officer Aubrey Hawkins, now survived by his wife, young son and mother.

The search for The Texas Seven spanned over six weeks and was said to be the largest manhunt in U.S. history involving the FBI, ATF and U.S. Marshall and captured the attention of media networks round the clock.

Six weeks later on January 21, 2001, the convicts were captured one by one and two by two in Woodland Park, Colorado, except for

Larry Harper who shot himself in the head rather than surrender alive. The Texas Six were then extradited back to Dallas to face capital murder charges in connection with the shooting death of Police Officer Aubrey Hawkins.

Shortly after the death of her son, Jayne Hawkins, the mother of the slain officer, filed a wrongful death lawsuit against the Texas Department of Justice for "causing the prisoners to escape".

During one of several interviews in early 2001, Hawkins stated, "The truth is, the Texas prison system is in terrible condition. There are a lot of problems and they led directly to the prison break. When you give [prisoners] no hope whatsoever, you make desperados out of them."

Although we deeply appreciate the mother's summation, there is something far more sinister at work here than the wiles of an institution. The destruction of one's soul can begin from the time one is born.

The truth is, if Joseph Garcia had *half* the mother Officer Hawkins had, this conversation would not be taking place; a notion that might have repulsed the late officer's mother, yet is nevertheless true.

The story of Joseph Garcia is but a mild

example of the type of distress children endure every day in America.

Joseph Garcia did not write this book to glorify the crimes of The Texas Seven nor was it written to rail against the Texas prison system.

Please join us in the final chapter as we examine what went wrong with the life of Joseph Garcia and so many other inmates in America.

Selma Kerren.

Part I

"Can a woman forget her nursing child, and not have compassion on the son of her womb? Surely they may forget, but I will not forget you. You see? I have inscribed you on the palms of My hands. Your walls are continually before Me."

Isaiah 49:15-16

Chapter 1

Murder/Murder

November 6, 1996, was not only my birthday but also the first day of my trial. What did it all mean? The indictment against me read:

The State of Texas vs. Joseph Christopher Garcia: Murder/Murder. Intentionally and willingly caused the death of the deceased, (named withheld), with malice.

In less than four days, a jury of my peers found me guilty of first-degree murder. I listened in disbelief as Judge James E. Barlows, the retired sit-in judge for Sid Harl, passed sentence over me.

"Joseph Garcia, I hereby find you guilty of murder by a trial of your peers and sentence you to fifty years, to be served in the Texas department of corrections. Do you have anything you'd like to say?"

What could I say, what could anyone say? He should have just put a bullet right through my brain. I think my lawyer answered for me; I'm not sure.

"Good luck, Mr. Garcia," said Judge Barlows, and when my eyes met his, it seemed he knew I had gotten the short end of the stick. *Good luck Mr. Garcia.* That's all I've been hearing ever since. *Good luck Mr. Garcia.*

As they cuffed me and led me out of court, I passed by my wife and mother-in-law, the only two people who showed up in my defense. Then they chained me to a bus headed for Connally Maximum Security Prison, near San Antonio. I would not see civilization again for a very long time.

Two years later, my wife divorced me, both of us having lost hope that I would ever get out. I don't blame her; at least she held on for two years. Neither my wife nor mother-in-law was allowed to testify on my behalf as character witnesses. My lawyer said he saw no reason why they should. I took this to mean that I had no character.

So much had already gone wrong in my life and I was in a state of shock that the first day of my trial occurred on my birthday. Had I been predestined for prison, or was it some cruel Texas courtroom joke? *Please God help me in my tribulations. What else could go wrong?*

A Cry In The Wilderness

I'm guessing that November 6, 1971, was a day of great relief for my mother, Juanita Frances Trevino, also known as Sophia. During those nine months of heartburn and morning sickness, Sophia claims I kicked out her navel and caused it to become an 'outie'. Sometimes, she felt I was running a marathon in her stomach. She told me I was a unique baby; smart, observant and very fond of breast-feeding.

Many times, she and my step-dad, Louie Negron, would take noontime naps. When they awoke, they would find me out of my crib, wandering about the apartment. On one such afternoon, as my mother lay napping next to Louie, she woke up suddenly. My step-dad was yelling, "What the hell!"

It turns out I was sitting on his chest with my diaper off, playing with my poop.

My mother and step-dad could never figure out how I got out of my crib until they inspected the screws and bolts. It seems I had learned to escape at a very young age.

Although my true name is Joseph Garcia, my family always called me "George" because I was a very resourceful and curious child, just like Curious George, the monkey. Therefore, throughout this book I will be referred to as

"George" because that was my childhood name. It's always comforting to know one was named after a monkey.

As a bastard child, I took well to Louie Negron, my stepfather, but hardly ever saw him reciprocate. Louie Negron was a nurse in the United States Army. When I was two months old, he moved us to some base in New York where, over the next ten years, Uncle Sam turned me into a regular, government-issue, Brooklyn Yankee.

I really don't remember him teaching me much of anything, much less sharing the good times that a father and son should have. I was at all times treated by his entire family as an outsider and royal pain in the neck.

Soon, my baby sister Arlene came along. She was my best friend and the only person that ever truly loved me in this whole world.

It was not until I learned to read that I realized my last name didn't match the rest of the family. My mother, stepfather and baby sister where all referred to as the Negrons but I was the 'Garcia'.

This was very confusing and hurtful to my young mind. Although I asked my mother about it many times, she never bothered to explain.

"Louie is your father now and that's all that matters."

Still, I felt that something was wrong. It did explain why Louie never treated me like his own child the way he did Arlene. Therefore, I can honestly say that my childhood memories from birth to about age ten are not very good. I should have thousands of good memories but have none; most of them are painful.

My only fond memories are of Arlene, my beloved sister and best friend. I loved her more than anything in the whole world. I used to take care of Arlene and we did everything together.

As the younger sibling, she copied everything I did. During those years in New York, we would go outside and play with the other kids in the neighborhood. Some of the boys and I would jump off a landing six feet above the street. One day, I noticed a bunch of kids standing around in a huddle looking at something on the ground. I skipped over, expecting to see a squashed bug or something and instead found my little sister lying on the concrete grimacing in pain. She had tried to copy my six-foot jump, hit her head on the concrete and almost knocked herself out.

I yelled for my parents so loudly that day, Arlene was in the hospital within ten minutes.

This incident left a terrible scar upon my sense of responsibility as an older brother. My daredevilry had almost killed my baby sister.

Another time, I had nearly gotten both of us killed. It was Saturday morning and I was cooking Arlene a fine breakfast of fried potatoes and eggs.

"George," she chided, "Do you even know what you're doing?"

"Of course I do, what d'ya think I am, stupid?"

"Well, George," she smarted back, "I think you're a really big dummy and you should wait for mom to wake up!"

But I didn't listen. Louie and Sophia awoke that morning to the kitchen blazing on fire. Arlene and I sat on the couch watching the unfolding comedy as mother and Louie ran about like Abbot and Costello, trying to put out the fire.

Me, myself and Arlene...we did everything together.

Chapter 2

Running For The Kools

It's now 1981 and I'm ten years old.

I don't recall my mother and Louie ever fighting much, at least not abusively. I think what eventually separated them was their mutual addiction to drugs.

I came home from school one day and my mother was packing our bags, just hers and mine. Arlene stayed with Louie.

Being so abruptly separated from my sister Arlene for the first time in my young life made me feel empty and lonely, but most of all I was truly lost without her.

My mother and I returned to San Antonio, Texas, probably the biggest mistake she ever made for the two of us. I was only ten; how was I to know the utter chaos that would enter my life over the next few years.

In San Antonio, we imposed upon my

maternal grandmother, two uncles and a cousin, who lived in a tiny house. My grandfather, Frank Trevino wasn't home when we arrived. He was an adulterer who regularly went to spend time with his 'first family'. He never married my grandmother because he was already married, spending time, as he called it, with both women and taking care of his children on both sides. Our side of the family was considered to be 'the black sheep' by the 'other family'. My grandmother allowed this man to play the Mormon polygamist in every aspect of their relationship.

Once in San Antonio, my mother slipped into the twilight zone and swiftly brought me in as the unwilling cast member of her daily dramas. Our lives had taken a dramatic turn from middle-class to rock bottom depression.

To top it off, my mother abandoned me, without food and money, at my grandparents' house to cope with their constant insults. Every time I put some of their food into my mouth or sat gingerly on the edge of their sofa, they let me know about it.

Where is Sophia? Why isn't she here? Why does his mother never pay any money to care for the boy? Why should we take care of him? He's not our responsibility!

You must understand, by now my mother was a heroin addict and had more important things to do with her money than buy food for me to eat; and I, ever faithful to my mother, wasn't about to tell them any of it.

My Aunt Sylvia did most of the complaining in rapid-fire Spanish, as though I didn't know what she was saying. As a matter of fact, I spoke Spanish fairly well. Grandmother Negron back in New York refused to speak to anyone unless it was in Spanish. Consequently, she spanked me routinely whenever I spoke to her in English. To this day, they never knew I understood every word they ever said.

Many times I wished I couldn't understand them. Words can hurt when you need someone to take care of you, but as with most things, I kept quiet and protected my mother.

After months of this humiliation, my mother and Louie suddenly made up. He had gotten a transfer, came down from New York with Arlene and we all moved into a San Antonio apartment on Broadway Street called La Capries.

There are no words to describe what it was like for me to see Arlene again. I do believe that for a short time, those were the happiest days of my life. Everything else simply ebbed away into nothingness by comparison; even my parents' heroin addiction seemed insignificant during those days. My mother had gotten a job at the Chinese restaurant up on the corner while I took care of Arlene after school. It seemed things were starting to really look up.

One Saturday morning, I was watching cartoons in our little San Antonio apartment when I learned something about Arlene that tore me in two.

Remember, Arlene was not only my sister, she was also my best friend, the only one I had ever belonged to. I loved her so much that I even beat up my best friend, Papito, one day back in New York because he threw an ice-packed snowball at her. Sometimes I can still hear her call my name.

On this particular Saturday morning, I heard a loud thumping noise coming from our back bedroom, which persisted for about two minutes. I was not alarmed when I heard Arlene cry out my name. I got up, sauntered unsuspectingly to our room twirling my bubble gum with one finger and there was Arlene, slumped on the floor. She was holding onto the edge of the bed with her face torn in pain.

"George!" she cried again in a small, frightened voice. "Get mom and dad, I can't get up!"

At first I thought she was joking. *C'mon Arlene, cut it out!* On many prior occasions back in New York, I had seen Arlene jump, kick, roll over and do cartwheels so why should I have taken her seriously this time?

"Shut up, come on, you're gonna' miss the cartoons!"

This time she began to cry, "Please George, get mommy and daddy!"

That's when my heart fell. The memory of my little sister sprawled out on the streets of New York flashed before my eyes and I took off running to my parents' bedroom.

"Arlene can't move, dad! Arlene can't move!"

Louie Negron crashed through the door and ran past me as my mother tried to come to her senses. Down the hall, Louie called out to Sophia and then she too ran past me. Louie quickly carried Arlene to the living room couch and we trotted after him with a heightened sense of urgency.

Then, my mother grabbed me by the shoulders and told me to get her purse. I ran and did as she asked, thinking there was medicine inside her purse, medicine to fix up my sister good as new. Instead, she took out a twenty-dollar bill and told me to run to the store for a pack of Kools.

What? Confused, I ran the six blocks to the store, bought my mother's cigarettes and was back in less than five minutes. When I opened the door to our apartment, breathless, I heard only the television. Everyone was gone.

I sat on the couch crying with my mother's Kools in one hand and change in the other. It was one in the morning when my parents finally returned from the hospital. They found me still sitting on the couch clutching the Kools. How could they have left me behind? They didn't even bother to explain that my sister was now paralyzed and dying.

Arlene was to stay in the hospital for a very long time after that. No one told me that my sister had terminal cancer, and when they finally did, I thought I would die of grief.

The cancer had completely paralyzed the right side of her body from the neck down, leaving only partial movement to her left extremities.

That whole day and night, all I could think was…*It must be my fault, it's all my fault.* And by the way they had left me behind I figured it must be true.

Chapter 3

Angel

Two months after Arlene's collapse, my mother and Louie separated again. Again she packed and moved us into a small San Antonio house on Theo Street, a block from my grandmother's house, way too close for my comfort if you ask me.

No one could figure out how my mother was able to finance all these sudden relocations on minimum wages but I'm sure if you try really hard, you could figure it out. Again I was separated from Arlene and again I was uprooted.

Since my mother was never around, she could have saved herself tons of money by just dropping me off at any number of doorsteps, but rather than face the firing-range of questions regarding her whereabouts and activities, she took to stashing me away in dank little apartments for weeks on end, with little food in the house and no one to look after me.

Now that I'm an adult, I look back on those days with amazement. Although I had no one to supervise me by the age of eleven, I was such a disciplined little kid. I would come home from school to an empty apartment, do my homework and then go out to play. Whoever heard of such a thing!

I would go to the neighborhood park until it closed at nine o'clock and then go home to an empty apartment. Sometimes my mother was there, sometimes not. Sometimes, I would simply find a note on the fridge…'*Be back later*…which usually meant the following week.

On days when my mother went missing, I would walk over to grandmother's house on the next block. By now, she actually gave me some food to eat without reading me the riot act. It was during one of those times that my grandmother started to become my friend and would chatter about all sorts of interesting things.

One day, she said, "George, I just realized something. Your mother is doing the same thing to you that she did to her first three children."

Excuse me, what did she say? That's right, I had three estranged siblings somewhere in the world that I never knew about. Grandmother told me that my mother was first married to a man named Daniel Garcia who was also in the United States Army, stationed in San Antonio. My mother actually had three school-aged children by him whom she abandoned because she was pregnant by another man, and it was me she was carrying. Oh great, more guilt-o-grams to deal with.

Grandmother told me that Daniel Garcia was not my biological father either, and that I was merely given his name at birth. There was yet a third man in the picture. My grandmother saw the distress on my face and finally told me all about Pops.

"George, you look so much like your real father!"

"You know my real father, grandma'?" My eyes popped out at this announcement.

Angel Luis Bermudez stood six feet, two inches tall at two hundred pounds and was a very handsome man who carried himself with much class. He was also in the service and my mother had left her first family for him. He was the man who had gotten my mother pregnant but grandmother said Angel Bermudez was a very good man so naturally I felt compelled to ask, "Then, *why* did he leave me?"

Grandmother answered that Sophia had run him off. She was not able to commit to him and was still with Danny Garcia, the father of her first three children. Angel Bermudez finally had enough and split while my mother fell back to Danny Garcia, but not for long.

Since Danny was still in the United States Army, he agreed to put his last name on my birth certificate to alleviate my mother's financial situation, after which I'm sure Danny Garcia's government paychecks became a little plumper to accommodate the additional child. It's nice to know one's worth, at least for a few weeks.

Shortly after that, my mother left Danny Garcia and took off with Louie Negron.

After discovering my sordid family origins during the eleventh year of life, I vowed to my grandmother that if I ever saw my real father, I would punch him in the stomach and then I would come live with him forever.

During those afternoons of discovery in my grandmother's kitchen, Arlene was still in the hospital and I missed her very badly. I kept asking for someone to take me to visit her but everyone's response was always the same. *She's doing real' good George; she'll be home soon.* And that was the end of it.

I wish I could declare that my mother was the picture of the doting parent pouring over her dying, paralyzed child at the hospital seven days a week but she wasn't. I do know that my mother loved Arlene, when she was straight, and would have *liked* to visit her. Does that count?

Pardon me, what's that you say? Am I making excuses for my mother? Go ahead, call me a mama's boy.

Chapter 4

'Be Back Later

Half a year must have passed when Arlene was finally released from the hospital because I was much taller. Although she had completed her chemotherapy treatments, Arlene was now confined to a wheelchair. She came to live with us and I can't tell you how happy I was.

My stepfather, Louie Negron, worked all day while my mother was now preoccupied with her full-time career as an executive, professional heroin addict. She came home only on occasion to assume responsibility for her crippled child, who was now nearing the death-grip of leukemia. So, I took it upon myself to care for my sister as if she were my own child. I cooked for Arlene, washed her, brushed her hair and tucked her into bed at night.

During the day she attended special-needs classes and after school I took her to the park where we would talk for hours and get fresh air.

During those days, Arlene told me everything that had happened to her from the time she collapsed. She said that even though the chemotherapy treatments had caused her a great deal of pain, she had made friends with the other children at the hospital who were sick just like her.

Arlene told me how they had group discussions, which helped her to better understand her cancer. Because of these discussions, she was no longer afraid to die. Arlene and the other children played a lot of games and her favorite was bowling. Apparently, she had become a pro' and could beat me anytime. Even though chemotherapy had caused Arlene a lot of pain, she said it hurt more being separated from me.

"Don't worry kiddo," I reassured her, "I'm here now and no one's ever gonna' separate us again!"

"You' damn right!" she smacked back like a blackjack dealer smoking a cigar.

Then one day when we were in the park, out of the clear blue sky, she said, "George, you know I'm gonna' die soon, right?"

That's when I blew my stack.

"Shut up Arlene! You're not gonna' die! What are you talkin' about?"

"My sickness, George, the doctor said … "

"I don't care what the doctor said, you're not gonna' die!"

I was shouting at her now with thoughts of Arlene lying on the concrete rising up to torment me. Then I started to cry. Deep inside, I knew she was right. Heck, she was such a smart aleck who had been right about everything else, why should this time be any different?

Arlene was mentally very sharp and strong at heart. She had accepted that her cancer would very soon claim her life just as it did her privilege of walking, but I had yet to come to terms with any of it. Once she left this world, I knew I would truly be alone.

"Don't worry George, I promise you when I get to heaven, I'll take care of you."

God, I hated it when she talked like that. What was I going to do without her? Didn't she understand she was all I had?

Toward the end of 1981, it became perfectly clear where my mother had run off to all those times. She had started dating a man named Papo Calo. He was severely involved in guns and illegal narcotics-trafficking which, to my mother, must have seemed like the never ending ice-cream truck of her dreams.

On one rare occasion when she came home,

my mother took Arlene and me to visit a certain man and woman across town who were also heavily involved in trafficking. It was the first time I would ever know true hatred.

While we were at their house, my mother suddenly stood up and announced that she and Papo Calo were going to the store.

'*Be back later…*

Three days went by and she still had not returned.

I brought with us our pet, a little grass snake that I kept in the pocket of my shirt. Arlene and I had found him a few weeks earlier in the park and we were more than happy to invite him into our little family. Arlene named him Slippy Sammy and he was about to die.

On the third day of our abandonment, we were playing outside this strange house, still waiting for our mother to 'be right back'. When we looked up, a police car had pulled up in front of the couple's house. When I saw the police, my mind *snapped* for the first time in my life. I knew what was going to happen next, had been expecting it for months, and dreaded the moment since I was old enough to reason.

I was so enraged and upset that I took Slippy Sammy out of my pocket and threw him against a brick wall, killing him instantly.

The woman inside the house had called the police and told them my mother had not returned after three long days and that she could no longer take care of us. Of course she couldn't, not with Arlene's condition, and by now both of us would be missed at school.

The police had come to take Arlene and me to the San Antonio children's shelter, something I had dreaded all my life. It was, in fact, my healthy dread of being fostered out which motivated me into covering up for my mother all those times but now the jig was up. Somehow I knew, once you went in, you could never get out. The heart remains fostered one's whole life.

It was not until my fifteenth birthday that I finally found out what happened to my mother, well, sort of. She and Papo Calo had driven down into Mexico to make a drug pick up. While Papo Calo was out doing the deal, my mother fell asleep in the car, was rudely aroused from her nap by Mexican police and swiftly arrested for drug trafficking.

I never found out how she scored her release from a Mexican prison (like trying to shift the earth from its axis of symmetry) but all you need is one cop on the take lookin' to make some extra cash.

Our first night at the shelter was a living

nightmare for Arlene and me. Since the place held boys and girls, there were separate sleeping sections. I argued for hours with the social workers not to separate us. I told them Arlene required special medical and emotional attention that only I, her true caretaker, could provide, but they wouldn't listen.

I even swung at the staff several times to stop them from separating us. Because I became violent, they secluded me in a separate area for hours on end. Hours after lights went out, I could hear Arlene still crying, calling me from the other room. The staff had locked the door of the boys' room so I couldn't get to her. But don't forget, when I was a baby, I had unhinged an entire crib. How was some juvenile door going to stop me from getting to Arlene?

However, it turned out that I didn't have to unhinge the door. As I lay there pretending to be asleep, the woman attendant had inadvertently left the door unlocked later that night. Once she walked away, I got up and tiptoed into Arlene's room where she was still crying.

Those sons of ### didn't even try to calm her down and just left her there, crying to the point of exhaustion. I climbed into her bed and waited for her to drift off to sleep.

As Arlene slept, I lay there next to her also

crying because I knew it was all over. Arlene and I would soon be farmed out and who knew what kind of caretakers we would get. Would they beat us, molest us, lock us in a closet? Arlene and I were not stupid; we knew what was out there.

I cried because I knew that her last few months of life would soon be taken away from me and they would never let me be there when she died.

My thoughts wandered away then, over the trees and rooftops of San Antonio, over the houses and happy homes I had seen from a distance all my life. Once in a while, I would look into their windows and see Christmas trees ablaze with color, surrounded by golden presents. I would see boys and girls at the park with snacks and toys and clean clothing. Shiny cars would drive up to the entrance; mothers would run up to them, give them a big hug and take them home to a happy house.

And I wondered how come some kids were born into happy homes and some kids were not? Why were some kids so important and others not? It was something I just never could figure out.

Looking back, I knew that none of those other kids had giant, adult-size problems like me. I had just turned twelve. Was I supposed to know how to handle the stack of cards dealt out to me?

That next hour, the woman attendant rushed over to our bed. She must have noticed I was not in the other room. To her credit, she made no gesture to remove me. She saw that the crying little girl was now fast asleep and that I truly was her appointed guardian, so she turned and walked away.

I didn't sleep at all that night trying to figure out a way to keep my promise to Arlene.

Don't worry kiddo, I'm here now and no one's ever gonna' separate us again!

Part II

"And there is no creature hidden from His sight, but all things are naked and open to the eyes of Him to whom we must all give account."

Hebrews 4:13

Chapter 5

El Chapolin

At the children's shelter, days turned into weeks. Arlene and I anxiously expected our parents to come and get us at any moment but Sophia and Louie were nowhere to be found.

By now, we had our schedule down to a pattern. It became alarmingly clear with every passing day that the staff of this children's home could no longer accommodate Arlene's special needs, of which I was the only self-professed, resident expert.

Also clear was the fact that they were engaged in the avid pursuit of placing Arlene into foster care and separating us for good. But how would they accomplish this and get past me was the question? They were wicked, these people, very wicked.

One morning after breakfast, all the children were led into the television room. It was the normal routine, nothing out of the ordinary. I rolled Arlene's wheelchair over to our usual spot in front of the television and settled in after which I proceeded to hand her the cookies one by one. One of the few tasks I allowed the staff to do without my supervision was to bathe Arlene and take her to the restroom. Other than that, I was on them like a bad suit.

On this particular morning, I allowed the staff to take her to the restroom. I was fixated on a television show that I liked very much called *El Chapolin*, a Spanish sitcom for children our age. After the show ended I came to my senses, looked around and suddenly realized Arlene had missed the entire show.

I ran around all over fully expecting to find my sister laughing and playing in another room somewhere but the more I searched, the more alarmed I became. Waves of dread flooded over me as I ran from room to room and I became angrier by the minute.

I bolted upstairs to our sleeping quarters, searched the dining room, the kitchen and hallways; I even ran outside into the yard. Then, I ran through the whole building a second time and still no sign of my sister. It was no use; I knew what they had done. Arlene was gone.

I had dropped my guard for just one minute and they stole my sister away from me. I went upstairs and sat on my bed defeated for an hour, praying to God that He would bring her back to me. Then, a female staff attendant walked into the room and sat on the opposite bed.

"George, we had to do it. Arlene needs special care, something we aren't equipped to do here. I hope you can understand there was no other way."

That was all she said and then she left the room. No promise that I could see her real soon, no assurance that she would be all right, no hint as to what would happen to me now. Just a cold 'hope you can understand'.

Yeah, I understood, all right. I understood that I hated this simpleton woman and her sensible psychobabble, I understood that they had just separated me from the only family I ever had and I understood things would never be the same again; but I said nothing. Tear after tear came then and tormenting thought after thought; Arlene was alone now and so was I.

I imagined how she must have tried to scream as they carried her away. Did they have to hold her mouth shut? Did they drug her milk? I cried until nightfall and eventually fell asleep, exhausted.

I awoke the next morning to an empty room. I had missed breakfast and was sure it was closer to lunchtime. I pulled myself together, knowing I couldn't just lay there forever.

I fell into my normal routine and put on a change of clothing with my mind crunching like a cash register, thinking of ways to escape, *kah-ching*, thinking of ways to get out, kah-ching, the bright red exit sign in the hallway, *kah-ching*, how tempting, how fitting. Yeah, that's it, just push the handle and walk out, *kah-ching*.

My train of thought was broken then by two grown-ups walking past me in the corridor discussing business of their own. It was lunchtime and I sure was hungry, so I put my plans aside for the moment.

Can't run away on an empty stomach.

A month had passed and the thought of running away turned into just another whistle in the wind, as was the thought of simply burning down the building.

With each passing day, I became more depressed. I had not only tasted of intense hatred for the first time in my life but now, it seemed, I would also battle depression. I'm no expert but I think that's what it was. It was like walking around half dead every day with my whole being wracked in pain from the inside out. I know for a fact, that if all that pain entered a herd of pigs, they would stampede off a cliff and commit suicide. Sound familiar?

No one in my family called or visited me during those long months nor did any of them bring me updates about my sister. Later I learned they hadn't gone to see her either. Amazing!

My appetite for food had diminished down to nothing and so did my need for social interaction. The destruction of my soul was now well under way. It was all so predictable, so textbook.

Then, one day God only knows how many months later, the supervisor of the children's home suddenly announced that I was going to visit Arlene! Perhaps there was hope after all that I might be reconciled with my beloved sister. That next afternoon I walked into Arlene's foster home and was met with another collection of anguish altogether.

The foster parents told me she had not come home from school yet. This gave me the opportunity to walk around their house and give them my boot camp, white-glove inspection and I made sure they saw me do it.

Yes, I had to admit they cut muster. They were very kind people with three children of their own and, to my relief, were generous with their stories of Arlene. They even told me how fond my sister was of me and went so far as to disclose that she 'couldn't stop' talking about me!

How much I wanted to cry in that house. Their accurate description of my very own sister and her love for me only caused me to suffer all the more, and it made me angrier than ever.

Please God, please let me live here with Arlene and these nice people; please don't make me go back to that place.

Then, I heard the school bus pull up and I became very excited. I told the foster parents to make no mention of me and to let my visit be a surprise.

I watched through the crack of the open door frame as the bus driver lowered Arlene's wheelchair by crane. From my very first sighting of her, I could see she was already running her mouth. Never the boring conversationalist, she would cuss you out like a New York City cab driver if you ever crossed her up.

As the crane of the school bus lowered her to street level, I could see that she was clean, well fed and happy. Her wheelchair rolled closer and closer to the house and I finally heard what she was chattering about.

"You know what? I put that boy in his place. How dare he talk to me as if he had a brain!" She was on a roll then. "I told him George would beat him up if he wuz' here 'cause I was tired of wastin' my breath!"

Apparently, she had gotten into an argument with a boy on the bus. As she rolled through the front door, chattering endlessly, I snuck up from behind and pushed her chair into the living room.

Then she became quiet and said, "I wish George were here."

By then I was crying so much I was surprised she hadn't heard me standing right behind her, so I bent forward and with a whisper I said, "I'm right here my love."

My love...that's what our mother used to call us on a good day, only she never meant it like I did. As I turned her chair around to face me, Arlene was already crying and I think I must have fallen on her.

I should say again that I truly respected those foster parents. During my entire visit at their house, they never once interrupted us and watched only from a safe distance. They even allowed me to take Arlene for a walk around the block all alone just like old times. We hugged and kissed so much out in public I'm sure that onlookers didn't know what to think.

The foster parents had set up a tent for us out in the back yard and we had our own private slumber party. As we lay together that night, side by side, Arlene wiped the tears from my eyes. She told me that all this would soon be over and then she would be able to take care of me. I knew what she meant but I refused to listen to her nonsense.

"Arlene, why do you always keep telling me stuff like that? I'm tired of talking about it."

"I just want you to be strong, George. Promise me one thing, when you grow up, promise me that you and your wife will have lots of kids so you won't ever be lonely."

When she said this, it tore through my heart. I guess she could see how staggeringly lonely I was without her and this was the only solace she could offer in her little girl's logic. And yet, as she wiped away my tears, I saw all too clearly that her words were very sage, very true. Arlene would soon die and I would have to find someone to replace her.

I was happy during those brief hours with Arlene but equally sad. I knew that by morning, I would once again have to say goodbye and endure the grinding motions of separation, and who knew for how long this time. I wanted to tell Arlene I would come and visit again very soon but could no longer keep my promises so I said nothing.

I awoke the next morning with Arlene studying me intently. There was a mischievous smile on her face as she watched her older brother sleeping.

"Well, what're you smiling at me like *that* for?" I said, feeling awkward and rubbing my face.

"Did you know that you talk in your sleep?"

"Do not!"

"Do too! And that's why I'm smiling at you, you big dummy!"

Arlene never told me that morning what I said in my sleep. Instead, she threatened to hold it against me as she had so many times before, if I didn't perform her every unbridled wish.

That girl knew just how to rope me down. One time, I had accidentally cut up the entire living room carpet with ice skates. My step-dad had spent hours laying down this brand new carpet and I ruined it in less than fifteen minutes. When my mother finally noticed the slices all over the carpet, all hell broke loose. Arlene's face beamed with delight as it did on this morning. She always made sure I was heavily indebted to her.

Surrendering Arlene back into the care of her loving foster parents was for me the closest I've ever come to dying. She wiped the tears from my face again, assuring me we would be together soon but somehow I knew I would never see her alive again.

The supervisor led me away then and we waved at each other one last time. I love you forever, Arlene.

Chapter 6

Drug Deal Gone Bad

One day, as Arlene enjoyed one of her many happy days at the foster parents' home, Louie Negron finally decided to fly down from New York and pick her up. He took Arlene back to New York with him and put her under the able care of one Doctor Gamboa.

About the same time, my grandmother came to pick me up from the children's shelter and I went to live with her once more. I guess it took the adults in our family a good year to come looking for their two disenfranchised children because I was now entering junior high.

At least my grandmother's tiny, one-bedroom house on the south side of San Antonio was safe and warm.

By now my mother had negotiated her way out of the Mexican jail and eventually made another deadly, cameo appearance at grandmother's house, announcing she had rented a new place close by while singing the oracles of brand new beginnings…with Papo Calo, the known drug kingpin, mixed into the plan.

Just as I had settled down to a normal child's life with school, sports and friends, she barged in, packed me up and dragged me off once again. Needless to say, this was all very upsetting for me; living with my unstable mother was a nightmare.

During those fleeting times with my mother, I came home from school one day and there she was with Papo Calo, shooting up heroin on the couch. She was already so high, she didn't seem to care that I was standing right in front of her as Papo cooked up the smack, tapped her arm for a good vein, drew up the needle and eased it into her flesh.

Both of them nodded off then and looked as though they were dying. Their eyes rolled back into their heads and that frightened me terribly. I didn't know if this was a good thing or a bad thing.

Alarmed, I grabbed my mother, shook and slapped her but she didn't respond. *Should I call the cops? Should I call an ambulance?* Fear and anger compelled me to pick up all the narcotics on the coffee table and flush them down the toilet.

Who knows how many hundreds of dollars I flushed away that day, hundreds that could have been spent on food and school supplies for me.

It was during this time that I became intricately involved in the underworld of drugs. I had known about marijuana since the age of seven, thanks to my mother and her 'responsible friends'. Back in the 1970s smoking a joint was like religion. If you didn't have any pot you were considered sacrilegious; an alien intruder in the almighty temple of hemp.

Up to that time, I had never put a joint to my mouth but as any child of the temple high priestess will tell you, it was just a matter of time. And so, as a junior high freshman, I became inducted into the temple.

Around the same time, I picked up a tennis racket and found that beating a ball against a wall with sufficient force released incredible, pent up anger and believe me, I became exceptionally good at it.

My junior high school coach said I had raw form and a natural talent for the game. Tennis meant more to me than just a game. The deeply seeded roots of anger and indignation propelled me to take on my opponents with inordinate aggression.

In my mind, every poor kid that stepped onto the court was a predator, a non-person, a family member who betrayed me, a staff member who deceived me, a parent who threw me away. All of them had to be punished.

Tennis consists of six, four-point games, which equal a set. Most of the time, it's played three out of five or five out of seven.

For the record, during my sixth, seventh and eighth grades, I never lost a single set I played. I would walk onto a court with a clean slate and walk off with all eighteen or all thirty games in my back pocket. Every game I ever played was all about being separated from Arlene and it showed up on court.

You might have put it together by now that at the tender age of twelve I played vigorous sets of tennis totally under the influence of illegal narcotics. And with the way I attacked a tennis ball, it's a good thing I never took up racecar driving.

You're probably wondering how a twelve year old got enough money to buy marijuana. Well, I was lucky remember? My mother and I had Papo Calo, our resident fix man.

One morning I was changing the sheets on my bed when I noticed a hole in the foot of my box spring. Inside was a fat, one-pound bag of marijuana. Christmas arrived early that year.

At first, I was afraid to touch it. There had always been ample drug paraphernalia laying all around our gun-running, drug-trafficking household, enough to delight an ATF squad but now it appeared the mother load had laid a golden egg right there inside my bed.

Visions raced through my mind almost immediately. In the first, I'm out at the park impressing all my friends...*Party time, hey, hey!* In the second, I'm sitting in a Mexican jail with my mother.

I finally worked up enough courage to open the package. To my non-surprise, I found a pack of rolling papers inside. Concierge service, how thoughtful! So, I did what any other unsupervised, unkempt kid-at-risk would have done in my situation. That day I pinched some out, rolled a plump joint and smoked it just like I had seen dearest mummy do on so many occasions. The next day I pinched out a little more. Here a pinch, there a pinch, everywhere a pinch-pinch, and before too long, I realized I was in big trouble.

I had burned two known drug dealers in the

'hood and suddenly I was a marked child.

How would I explain this to my mother, the major drug dealer and Papo Calo, the gunrunner? Would they blind-fold me, drive me out to the desert and kill me execution style? Would they kidnap me and demand a ransom? How much time would I have before I got whacked?

So, I did the smartest thing I could think of; I waited a couple days until my mother got high and told her the truth. The result was almost disappointing.

"I know George, I know, don't worry," she giggled, amused. "I told Papo I smoked it, everything's okay."

Because her set of values were so irreversibly twisted by then, she actually thought it was cute that her school-age child consumed an entire pound of weed.

Had I been hungry one day and consumed one too many Krafts individually wrapped, cheddar slices, I'd get a smack across the head. In the matter of drugs, however, I was offered deep absolution by the high priestess of the temple of hemp. Such were the never-ending relationship dynamics between my mother and me.

Soon thereafter she again dropped me off at

grandmother's doorstep and disappeared. I guess she didn't want to share the herb.

By then, I was demonstrating the predictable, garden-variety set of behavioral problems that all abandoned, furious children display. My grandmother had special ways of dealing with me, which I found rather endearing. As long as she could still throw a shoe across the room, Troy Akeman style, or an axe for that matter, I tried not to upset her too much.

I kept my grandmother informed as to my whereabouts at all times and regularly left notes on the fridge telling her where I would be and when I'd be home. I had determined to always be a good boy and nothing like my mother. 'Don't know what went wrong.

I love you grandma'. Rest in peace.

Chapter 7

The Rich Man's House

Just as I was settling in over at grandma's house for the umpteenth time, the high priestess made another sudden and disruptive appearance at our door and forced me to leave with her again. This time, she had actually gotten a job working as a live-in nanny, of all things, taking care of a rich man's children.

What? Wait a minute. Let's go over that again. My mother would be taking care of a rich man's children? Right now, the obvious question is, how could my mother take care of other people's children if she can't even take care of her own? Good question.

This time around, living with my mother was actually not so bad. It seemed that after her arrest down in old Mexico, she had gotten a reality check, if only for the moment, was trying to clean herself up, and made an honest go of it, having even taken honest employment to make it work. And whenever she made the slightest effort to be a mother to me, I was more than happy to flush away all her sins.

Couldn't she see what she had done to me? By now, the pungent tea of suffering had seeped permanently into my soul. It was like being in a head-on car crash, rolling over and over down a hill from which there was no escape. Anger, rage, trauma, the sadness of her absence, lack of love, momentary joy and repeated disappointments were all trapped within me now, incapacitating my heart perhaps forever.

"George," my mother said a few weeks after we had settled in at the rich man's house, "I've brought you here because my boss is going to send us to New York for a vacation."

For a vacation? Well, how long had she been working there to earn a vacation so soon? And why would an employer obligate himself as to actually pay for our travel to New York?

I knew right away we were going to see Arlene because she was getting ready to die but why couldn't she just say that, instead of calling it a vacation?

Years later I concluded that to my mother, everything was a vacation, even watching her own child waste away. I would have to say, however, that when she told me about this plan, it was one of the happiest moments of my life.

It was all set. My mother and I would have dinner with her boss and his family that night and set off for New York the following morning. I remember that night so vividly as if it were yesterday. I was hours from seeing my Arlene and it felt as though I were dreaming.

My mother and I sat happily at the dinner table with her boss and his family, eating, chatting and laughing. At that very moment I realized for the first time how much older I was and how long I had been separated from Arlene. Again, I remembered the promise I made to her back at the children's center, the promise that stilled her crying, the promise that we would never be separated again. Failure to perform this promise suddenly made me feel sick.

Then something strange happened; an unwelcome wave of dread flooded over me. Suddenly everything seemed to float about in slow motion.

I looked around the table to see if anyone else had noticed it but they had not. Now, the twenty hours I would have to wait became an eternity. This dinner was supposed to be a happy occasion but something was just not right.

From that point forward, I could no longer eat. My gaze finally fell upon my mother chatting next to me but I couldn't understand anything she said. Had she read my mind at that moment, she would have heard me say, *I'm not coming back Mom, this time I'm staying with Arlene.*

Everyone at the table continued chattering about aimlessly but my mind had sunk into some deep foreboding. And then it happened. Then the phone rang.

My mother's boss got up from the dinner table and continued to gossip, shaking his head and making comical hand gestures as he walked over to the phone. *Hello?*

I watched the boss's face. He became alarmed and motioned for my mother to come to the phone. I don't think I was breathing at all then.

My mother took the phone and within three seconds pain tore across her face. Her eyes met mine and then she collapsed.

Everyone ran over and surrounded her but my eyes were transfixed on the dangling telephone. I got up, walked over and slowly picked up the receiver. On the other end, I heard a man's voice repeatedly calling my mother's name, over and over.

"Frances? Frances, are you there, Frances?" That was my mother's true name when she wasn't being a drug trafficker.

"Hello?" I said, "Who's this?" When I told the man my name he fell silent.

"George," he said, "I'm not sure if you remember me but I'm your family doctor here in New York, Doctor Gamboa."

"Yeah, I know you." He was the doctor who had treated Arlene when she first collapsed.

"George, I've been trying to get a hold of your mother for some time now but no one knew where she was. I'm sorry to be the one to tell you this George but Arlene, your sister...she passed away, son. She was buried last week. I'm so sorry..."

What was this man saying? Who was buried last week? It couldn't have been *my* sister! My mother said we were going to visit her tomorrow! Or had she known all along Arlene was dead? Is that why we were going to New York?

They told me I dropped the phone, walked over to the couch and sat down. The last person I saw was my mother's boss, weeping now and kneeling in front of me, trying to get my attention but I couldn't hear him. He drifted further and further away until he was gone. I guess that was when my mind split.

I was in the dark now, walking in the darkness but I could still hear and see. As I was walking, suddenly a gush of wind blew in front of my face. It was Arlene! It was the wind of her little-girl smell. I called out her name but there was no answer. Then, I saw a small light in the distance growing larger and larger, coming ever closer and then the light gave way to a carousel.

The carousel came as close as fifty feet from me and then it stopped. It was so bright that it cast a shadow on the two figures coming from around the side of it. The tall figure was pushing a little girl sitting in a wheelchair. It was Arlene. I couldn't move, I wanted to but I couldn't it. I stood frozen on that spot and could see Arlene waving and smiling.

"Don't be afraid George," she said, "I'm okay now, really I am."

Wait a minute! What kind of perfunctory joke was this? Christ promised there would be no more tears, no more disease, no more suffering in the Kingdom of Heaven. Why was Arlene still in the wheelchair? As if to read my mind, Arlene answered the alarm on my face and stood up from her wheelchair. Whereas she had not walked in years, she now stood up, smiling, glowing and walking toward me on her own. She walked easily and with the perfection of angels.

"George, it's alright now, you don't have to worry any more," she reassured me, smiling brightly.

"I'm sorry Arlene." My heart burst with regret. "I'm sorry I was so far away."

"It's okay George, you couldn't do anything about it. We always knew it would happen." Arlene spoke with her usual crisp logic, even from eternity. "Now I can live and keep my promise to you," she said. "I'll take care of you now."

"But I don't want that!" I protested with tears stinging down my face. "I want you back! I don't want you to leave!"

I was speaking as a young boy who had lost the only thing he ever loved, not fully realizing that Arlene was finally released from her confinement and suffering.

"I'll always be with you George, I love you forever! Take care of mom, okay?"

Now my legs began to move again. I took a step toward Arlene but she drifted away. I ran after her but it was no use, she drifted backward, faster and faster like a balloon into eternity.

"Let me come with you Arlene!"

"You can't," she called down. "It's not your time yet, George! I love you!"

"I love you too, Arlene!"

And then I stopped running after her. The light got smaller and smaller and then it disappeared. I was now in the dark again and saw other lights. I tried to focus on them until the images became clearer. It was a doctor shining a light into my eyes.

"Joseph...can you hear me?" he prodded, calling me by my true name.

The rich man's family physician had rushed over to the house and determined I had sunken into a catatonia of sorts, which lasted upwards of six hours. At one point, the doctor feared I would never snap out of it but Arlene saw to it that I did, fulfilling her promise to watch over me.

I was incensed that my mother could not be found for weeks on end, not even to bury her own child.

Lying there under the care of the rich man's doctor, I thought about how I would live without Arlene. *I'll always be with you George.* I heard it again and smiled. Then I began to cry. *I love you too Arlene, I love you too.*

Arlene once told me, "George, if you never

tell people your feelings, they're never gonna' learn from your mistakes." Then she burst out laughing.

It took me a while but eventually I got the joke. I was her older brother but she was also my mentor, my salve and my bearings; even if she did make fun of me.

I don't know what it was that I saw that day. Whatever the case, Arlene is no longer among us but the memory of her might bring a tear of calm resolve to anyone who reads this.

At this writing, the State of Texas wants a pound of flesh from me and they will have it soon enough. These memories, however, are my emotional treasures that they can never take from me nor bury.

Chapter 8

Uncle Johnny

Even though Arlene was now gone, our travel plans didn't change. We arrived in New York City the following afternoon and I felt awkward as we rode the elevator of my cruel step-grandmother's building; the same one who would smack you if you talked to her in English, the same one who resented my ever being born.

My mother, who was always brash and aggressive, was afraid to approach the door on this day and that is why she made *me* go and knock on the door while she cowered behind the corner. No doubt, she knew how guilty she looked, having missed her own child's funeral by weeks. Whatever the case, my mother was finally afraid of something...the proverbial mother-in-law.

There I stood as the bastard child forced to knock on the door of some grumpy, old woman who hated me and yet a strange new strength rose up within, as if I would punch someone in the gut if they dared to cross me. Damn all of them for leaving us in that children's shelter, and damn all of them for separating us.

Louie Negron, my estranged stepfather, opened the door and we stood looking at each other, O.K. Corral style. He expected me to address my elder first but I said nothing. Surprised that I didn't flinch, *who's the man now?* he finally spoke.

"Your mother…where is she?"

"Hiding behind the elevator." I was in no mood to cover up for her this time.

My step-grandmother had converted the smallest bedroom inside the apartment into a hospital room for Arlene, complete with a medical bed and apparatus, which was still set up when we walked in. I climbed up onto the bed and lay there for a few minutes, taking in the ever-present scent of my baby sister.

My step-grandmother iced my mother down with eyes like an ice pick to the extent we had to leave quickly, so we went on a ferry ride leading up to Staten Island. It was good for me to get out of that death house and into the fresh air and sea spray of my old hometown. Upon our return to the building, Louie Negron's brother was there to meet us.

Uncle Johnny was genuinely happy to see

me. He took me out and told me all about Arlene. He said Arlene had never stopped talking about me right up to the very end. Apparently, she drove them all crazy.

"George," Johnny grinned at me, "She loved you more than anybody else. She told me to tell you that." And then, Johnny actually hugged me. He said, "I'm so sorry George."

At this point, I couldn't help but cry. I missed Arlene terribly by then, and still do with the same level of anguish.

He had no excuse to offer, however, for the sorry behavior of his brother, who had taken Arlene away from me and left me behind at the San Antonio shelter. He agreed with me that his brother should never have done that. He said it was Arlene's wish that they go and get me but they never honored it. Arlene was a dying little girl; what would it have cost them to grant her that one last wish?

Uncle Johnny liked me so much I began to wonder if he might like to have me come and live with him.

That was the last time I ever saw my Uncle Johnny. Shortly thereafter, he died in a motorcycle accident that broke his neck.

The accident that killed him took place within a few months of Arlene's death. Both deaths were too much for me to take and I don't think I ever recovered. Who knows?

My step-grandparents moved to California and before too long, forgot all about their misery on the warm beaches of the West Coast amid the sunshine and palm trees.

Shortly after that, my mother took off and abandoned me on the streets of New York City.

Chapter 9

An Afternoon With the FBI

My mother and I didn't fly back to San Antonio as you might have guessed but stayed on in New York; so much for the supposed vacation from her new job. In fact, she had no intentions of ever returning to the rich man's house.

Why should she? She had stolen jewelry from the man's wife right before we left. All I got from the take was an expired plane ticket and the cold, hard streets of New York City.

It's now 1983 and I'm almost thirteen. Nothing much had changed. I was again left on the doorstep of total strangers, this time in the Bronx, the hardest city in the world.

Remember Papo Calo? Well, it just so happened that ole' Papo's family also lived in New York; needless to say, we ended up staying with them. My mother, in true form, continued to see Louie, secretly of course, while spending time with Papo the gunrunner.

Again I didn't see my mother for days on end, which must be very tawdry to listen to by now, except for one new twist. This time her negligence had sunken to hysterical depths. She actually failed to enroll me in school!

During my lone haunt of the Bronx, I would occasionally walk across the street to the public school and interact with the other kids during their recess. I felt confident that none of the teachers ever saw me come and go, so I pushed my luck one day and followed the kids into the atrium to see a movie. The principal, however, spotted me within minutes and very quietly knelt down beside me.

"Son, mind if I have a talk with you?"

I was busted. He took me into an anteroom and questioned me with the usual who, what, why, where and when gig. It seems they had indeed noticed me at every recess and were concerned as to why I was not in school. As always, I protected my mother like a good Puerto Rican son and told them we had come to bury my sister, but was careful not to disclose any details as to my mother's gross negligence or drug addiction. Besides my sister's death, it was the greatest disappointment of my life to watch on as my mother actually abandoned me to the brutal streets of New York City with no food, money or shelter.

The kind principal gave me free license to come and go during recess periods and to watch movies with the other kids, based on his understanding that my mother and I were "just visiting". Before too long, however, he may have found out the truth and taken steps, so I never went back.

A week elapsed before my mother finally showed up at the Calo household whereupon she handed me a crumpled, expired plane ticket and some money. This time, she sat on the stairs of the fire escape fleeing for her life.

"I have to go now, George," she said, matter-of-factly with one leg out the window.

"People are looking for me. Here, take the ticket and some money. If I don't show up in a month from now, get a flight back to San Antonio and call up grandma' to come pick you up from the airport. Here's a fifty to renew your ticket. Gimme' me a kiss."

She pursed her lips as if I were a Los Angeles lunch date and then disappeared. No sooner had she fled, there came a knock at the front door.

"Who is it?"

"FBI, open up."

"I'm not allowed to open to strangers."

"FBI, open up now!"

"Yes, how can I help you?" I called through the door.

"This is the FBI, we're looking for Francis Trevino."

"I'm sorry but there's no one here by that name, this is the Calo residence."

I was very professional in the business of protecting my mother and considered myself her chief of staff but the FBI continued to knock.

"What do you want?'

"FBI, open up!"

I opened the door then but only after I made sure my mother had plenty of time to skip out the back. Two suits stood before me doing what they had dreamed about when they were kids, flashing their badges (it's why they get up in the morning). Immediately their eyes scanned the inner caverns of Papo Calo's apartment for their fugitive.

"Son, we saw the woman come into this building."

"And?" I smarted back. "Doesn't mean she's here now!" Then I went in for the kill. "And besides, my dad said I'm not allowed to open the door to strangers."

The one suit looked at the other suit, obvious that my guilt trip worked its magic.

"Sorry for bothering you son, have a nice day."

With that, they turned on their heels and left. What? That was it? I had just outsmarted two federal agents without so much as a contest. It's nice to know how your tax dollar is spent.

This was now the second time my mother and I had dodged law enforcement personnel. The first time was back in San Antonio when she came running home one day, breathless, demanding that I lock the door behind her.

"And whatever you do, don't let anyone in!"

"Don't let *who* in?" I questioned as she ran into the back of the apartment.

"Don't question me, just do what I say!"

A few minutes later, people were pounding at the door. *Police! Open up!* It was the police all right, with badges, guns and a warrant for my mother's arrest.

They kicked down the door and practically trampled me to the ground. I guess the cooking pot I swung at them didn't intimidate them in the least. *Get outa' the way kid!* They bolted everywhere throughout the house shouting in chorus.

Clear!…Clear over here! From room to room they ran…*Clear!*

Now, in my room was a closet with a pile of clothing five feet high. Well, isn't that what every kid's closet looks like? When they got to my room, they opened the closet door and *presto!* Sophia wasn't there. Or, was she?

One agent even moved about two feet of clothing out of the way and still no Frances Trevino aka Sophia Garcia Negron.

Eventually, they scratched their heads, confounded, and left.

"Mom," I whispered, when the coast was clear. "They're gone now, you can come out!"

She had indeed hidden beneath my five-foot pile of clothing.

"Now, aren't you happy that I clean my room a special way?"

She laughed and kissed me. Then she said, "I owe you one!" But she never paid up.

Chapter 10

The Boogieman

The Bronx was a whole other bag of apples, man.

During my stay in the Calo's fine broom closet I saw extremely violent things.

One night, Papo Calo's sister took all of us to meet her boyfriend, Frankie. We found Frankie sitting at the bus stop near his house drenched in blood. As we walked towards him, the darkness of night didn't reveal Frankie's present condition. He had gotten jumped by a gang and was severely beaten about the face and head with brass knuckles. It took over a hundred stitches to put Frankie back together again. I bet he was glad we came along.

Around the same time, I saw Papo Calo's brother grab a man in the neighborhood, put a nine-inch butcher knife to his neck and threaten to cut his throat. It turned out the man owed Papo's brother some money and was now trying to evade the issue. 'Can't say I blamed him; the entire family was crazy.

On the other hand, who was I to talk? My family was not without its moments. I am reminded of the time back in San Antonio when my mother first met Papo. My Aunt Sylvia came running into my grandmother's house in the early morning hours screaming bloody murder. I was asleep with grandma' in the back bedroom when Sylvia burst in.

"Mom! He stabbed Tito, he stabbed him!"

Once my grandmother managed to calm her down, Sylvia told us the whole story. Apparently, Papo, my mother's boyfriend had stabbed Sylvia's boyfriend, Tito.

Well, that's one way to meet your future in-laws, just stab one of them and blend right in. Sylvia was hysterical, with her makeup smeared across her face. Whatever happened at the nightclub no doubt involved the weekend stash of drugs. Papo had gotten upset with Tito and instead of talking out their differences like gentlemen they beat one another half to death.

Now, Tito held a black belt in Karate and Papo knew he could not compete with that, so he went to his car and got out his rusty pair of garden shears. Reasoning that the fight was now equal, Papo settled the matter by stabbing Tito with the garden shears.

A Cry In The Wilderness

It's always amazed me what women find attractive in men like Papo Calo. After all the evil she had seen Papo do, my mother continued to cling to him like a fly on sticky paper and for this reason our entire family pushed my mother away. My family might have been crazy but they weren't stupid.

Meantime back in the Bronx, shortly after I saw Papo's brother threaten to kill that man with a butcher knife, I saw another man murdered right in front of my face. At the tender age of thirteen, even I knew that I had seen too much for my age.

If you recall, the day my mother fled from the FBI on the fire escape, she had left me with fifty dollars for the express purpose of renewing my expired flight ticket. I ended up having to spend some of that on food, for which I make no apology.

With the fifty dollars almost gone I was now quite literally alone and stranded in New York with no way to get back to my grandmother's house in San Antonio.

During those days, another truant kid in the Calo building invited me to go to the park and I, showing off, offered to buy us both lunch.

As we turned the corner happily with brown paper lunch bags in hand, we heard a gunshot;

and that's when we saw the evening news a few feet away.

A young, Hispanic man was chasing a black man down the street. The Hispanic man leveled his gun, aimed and fired at the black man. The black man spun around and crashed into the front end of a screeching car. The driver took off, too afraid to stop. The momentum of the victim's body and the impact of the bullet caused the whole thing to look like something out of a stylized episode of Dukes of Hazard, only in this episode, the man didn't get up.

The victim slid off the car and hit the ground. I'm sure it was sheer adrenaline that kept him from dying on the spot. What was this about? A woman, or stolen property? Maybe a drug deal gone bad?

Valiantly, the shot man got up on all fours only to get knocked back down by a second bullet fired into his back. The incident was unreal. I stood transfixed, frozen to the ground. I turned to the left to look at my friend but he had taken off running down the street. So, I stood there clutching my sack lunch, trembling.

The Hispanic man now towered over the black man in the middle of a four-way intersection like some god who had the power to give life and take it away, and then he spoke.

"Turn over you ###!"

The gunman began to kick at the victim's feet. His voice was calm, too calm. He wanted the victim to look up at his face and play the stoic victim. That's when I thought, *Oh, I know, it's a movie! They're making a movie here!*

So, I looked around for the lights and the camera and the make-up lady but there weren't any. *Why do I have to keep seeing stuff like this?*

My young thoughts were soon interrupted. This afternoon horror matinee, to which I unwillingly occupied a front row seat, would not let me go. The leading man spoke again now.

"I said, turn around you piece of ###!"

I knew what was coming next. *Don't turn over man, please don't turn over!* However, as with every good horror flick, victims always do the opposite. The stupid girl always goes for a swim in the lake at midnight and the stupid guy always steps into the monster's trap. Later in the movie you find them hanging upside down in the barn.

By now, the black man on the ground was crying. He knew his life had come to an end. And so, resigning himself to his own death, he turned over, laboriously, with two slugs already in him. Without further exchange between gunman and victim, the next sounds I heard were three consecutive, high caliber shots fired straight into the victim's head. The shots ricocheted across the concrete canyons of the Bronx.

The victim's head exploded like a watermelon. A pink puff, brain matter and blood sprayed across the intersection. What seemed like an eternity actually transpired in less than a minute from the time we heard the first shot, to the final shot. In the distance, police sirens began to whine through the canyons, which made the shooter look up and take a step backward. And then he looked me right in the eye.

He was a young man of about eighteen or nineteen. My heart pounded so loudly then I was sure he could hear it. He was thin with short black hair and a pockmarked face. The thought of my own death didn't cross my mind. What did I care? I had just seen the brains blown out of a man's head. I could hear Arlene in my head. *Run, you dummy, run!* But it was no use. Besides, I had a brown paper lunch bag to protect me and I clutched it as if for dear life.

The shooter looked down once more at the lifeless body of the man on the ground, considering the pattern of the man's blown apart head. With police sirens drawing nearer, he looked at me again. Now, a grotesque smile sliced across his face. It was not the smile of an evil man. On the contrary, his smile was like the parent who sees his child doing something cute. *Aw, isn't that precious, look how cute he is when he's upset.*

I suppose I must have looked little and cute and silly, clutching my lunch bag as if it were a teddy bear. My innocence seemed to amuse the gunman. He knew I was paralyzed and that I couldn't move. The simple fact that he allowed me to live became a sort of sick bond between the two of us at that moment. We were cutting a deal, he and I. He allows me to live and I don't finger him in a line-up. *I scratch your back, you scratch mine, forget what you saw and I let you live. Okay son, okay kid?*

Once he saw that I understood him perfectly, he turned on his heels and ran back up the street, missing the cops by about three seconds. My new mentor, my new father, or whatever he was, ran away until I lost sight of him forever. Or did I?

I turned to look again at the splattered man on the street. He was still now, and dead. Finally, the numbness in my legs lifted. I turned and walked back to the empty shell of my room, trembling like a one hundred year old man. *It's just a bad dream, yeah that's it.*

I honestly didn't know what this life was all about. What was I doing here? Why am I here?

Lunch hour was over now. My very own

matinee horror show came complete with a front row seat and a personal message from the leading man. *Yeah, I got your message, loud and clear.*

After that, I called my grandmother in San Antonio and a caseworker came and got me.

I can still see him very clearly in my mind. His cadaverous, pockmarked smile would never allow me to forget. And so he remains the certifiable boogieman, the monster of my dreams.

Part III

"I will declare my iniquity.
I will anguish over my sins."

Psalms 38:18

Chapter 11

The Dad Gang

It's Christmas Day, 1995. I'm a fully-grown man now, age twenty-four, and somehow I survived. I've got a wife, a baby girl and bills I can't pay.

Just the day before, I was out with a friend named Bobby Lee Lugo at a garage party when we were attacked by a gang of middle-aged men. You've never taken a beating till The Dad Gang gave you one.

Bobby Lugo reminded me somewhat of my mother. He was ruthless, irresponsible, flamboyant and irrational but he was also my best friend. At this juncture of my life, anyone remotely more stable than my mother was a saint so I was still too young to process who was good for me and who was not.

Because Bobby was an impulsive individual he ignored my repeated warnings that day concerning a certain under-aged girl who was off-limits. Inside the garage party I pulled

Bobby over to the side and tried to warn him about this young girl. Typical of my irreverent friend, Bobby dismissed me with the wave of his hand as if to swat flies.

Later that night, however, as Bobby slow danced with the girl, her outraged father caught him by the scruff of the neck. Bobby then made the mistake of telling the girl's father to ### off and walk outside into the yard.

Now, the girl's father knowing he had just been seriously dis'd, left the party with a new Latino edge on his face. I told Bobby something was about to go down and I was getting out of there with or without him. This time he actually listened to me.

As we were making the rounds saying goodbye, it happened. Let me put it this way, Bobby and I barely made it out of there alive.

Six weeks later, I was standing in the shower looking down at the six-inch slash on my thigh, which was still trying to heal. It was on this day in the shower that I would never be the same again.

I suddenly realized how exposed I was and how shifting, dangerous and fleeting all of life can be. When you're a kid, you're preoccupied with hoping things will get better, but then you grow up to find that sudden events can be very final and very damaging.

A strange and distinct fear took possession of me that day in the shower. Or, had it been there all along and finally came home to roost? I couldn't tell which, but it made me shudder. It was different than being afraid when I was a kid, different than being assaulted by a gang. I believe you might call it mortal fear.

Don't get me wrong; I'm not that frail. I don't know anyone who could take on thirty, middle-aged Latino men at one time. (The girl's father had a lot of friends.) However, this individual actually produced a knife that managed to reduce me into a corner like one of those victims I had seen die in the street when I was a boy; only I lived to tell about it.

That day in the shower was the turning point for me; protecting my person against violence became my new preoccupation. I also continued to notice the glaring fact that not all people were dealt my kind of hand in life and by then, well, I'd kind of had it up to here.

Because I could not seem to free myself of the relentless cycle of danger and chaos, I began to fiddle with a knife of my own.

It was a butterfly knife. The butterfly was the direct link to all my childhood, kung-fu, super-hero fantasies. So I purchased the gleaming, stainless steel butterfly as a gift to myself and learned to master its intricacies, its openings and closings, and found strength in the sheer, icy, slicing sounds it made. Like learning how to ride a bike, you never forget its simplicity and precision.

The knife came complete with a carrying case that sat on your belt horizontally, making it a particularly quick draw. To produce the knife from concealment to ready-use could be as fluent and swift as you please, depending on your dedication to practice. And I certainly became the apt pupil of the butterfly.

Chapter 12

The Co-Worker

On the night of February 1, 1996, I made a decision that had never before entered my mind. Instead of leaving the butterfly knife at home, I actually went out wearing it into the night, not to use it but because it made me feel safe and secure.

My wife and I had been separated for some time and planned to officially get back together later that very week. During this separation, my Uncle Frank, his family and I were all staying at my grandmother's little house in San Antonio.

That night at 10:30 P.M. Uncle Frank and I drove up to Bobby Lugo's place of work, and I'll try to say this with a straight face, the Santa Rosa Mental Hospital.

When we rolled up, Bobby was just coming out and preparing to leave with some guy I didn't recognize. From the questioning look on his face, I could tell he had forgotten about our plans. Bobby said he made other plans with his co-worker to go to a nightclub called Piranhas, to have a couple of drinks and then go home.

My original plans with Bobby were not that different so I invited myself along and sensed no warnings of impending doom. The night's allotment was harmless enough: three guys going out to have a good time, nothing more. We would get a table in front of the dance floor, have some drinks, enjoy the music and then go home. We were what you might call the *Norms* of the sitcom *Cheers,* and there was nothing different about this evening than any other.

Bobby then jumped into his truck with the co-worker, a somber young man whose name has been omitted in respect of his family. We'll call him 'the co-worker'.

We all convoyed back to my grandmother's house to pick up my car. It was along this stretch that my Uncle Frank expressed his ill sense of something foreboding and he tried to discourage me from going out that night.

"George," he began, "Why do you have to go out tonight?"

"Why not Frank?" I spat back, "I haven't been out in quite a while, bro'."

After a two-year split, my wife and I would

be moving back together later that week so who knew when I'd be able to go out again. Besides, I needed to use the phone at Bobby's house to call my girlfriend, if you please, and tell her goodbye. (My grandmother didn't allow long distance calls placed from her telephone).

"It'll be good for me to go out," I explained to Uncle Frank. "And by Wednesday, I'll be back with the old ball and chain."

"Yeah I know," said Uncle Frank as if he hadn't heard a word I said. "But why don't you stay home tonight? We could get us a couple movies, a bag of weed and some beer; guy's night in, what do you say?" Uncle Frank's voice was strangely menacing.

"C'mon' bro, you sound like we'll never get to party again. It's just for tonight and then we' got the whole weekend. Tell you what Frank, give me one good reason why I should stay home, sans the beer, weed and movies."

As we pulled up to the front door of my grandmother's house, Uncle Frank sat there for a minute thinking.

Finally he said, "Have a good time George, but do me a favor, alright?"

"Sure, what?"

"Be careful bro'. I don't need you comin' home with another hole in you."

I smirked and jumped into my car. Following Bobby's truck, I thumbed my nose at Uncle Frank's warning and forgot all about it the rest of the night.

We arrived at the Piranha Club at about 11:45 P.M. It was there in the parking lot that I officially met the co-worker for the first time. When Bobby introduced me, I walked over to this newcomer, shook his hand and bantered about with him a little.

"It's nice to meet you man but hey, I warn you, if you hear us talkin' crazy, take no offense. Bobby and I go back a long way. We're best friends."

I meant this to be humorously competitive but the co-worker obviously didn't like the odd, friendly jab. He offered me a limp, cold hand, looked away and never said a word. I know that first impressions are crucial when meeting others and I have always tried to make a newcomer feel like a player on the team, but I felt an instant failure in securing our acquaintance.

Right from the start, I knew he was high on marijuana, could see it in his liquid eyes with the aroma of high-grade stash exuding from his person and Bobby's vehicle, and yet this was not the cause of my alarm concerning the co-worker. From the onset I could tell he didn't like me.

Inside the club we found a table near the dance floor, ordered drinks and settled in. The co-worker announced he was going to walk round and took off with a longneck Budweiser in his hand. I gave Bobby all the cash I had and he ordered two kamikaze shots, two Jack Daniel shots and five beers for each of us.

During our entire stay at the club, I saw the co-worker only two or three times still holding a longneck Budweiser but couldn't tell if that was the beer he started with or the umpteenth one, but I could see he was enjoying himself.

The bar was now closing and it was time for us to go home. We found the co-worker out front talking to some girl. One thing about Bobby Lugo, once he decided it was time to go he meant it and would leave you in the dust cloud if you didn't hustle to his program. And now the co-worker seemed agitated that we peed all over his Cheerios.

It was definitely a cold morning, cold enough to see my own breath streaming from my mouth. On the way back to my car, I turned and looked again at the co-worker. I couldn't quite put my finger on it. He seemed repellent, for lack of a better word, not a team player.

Five minutes down the highway, Bobby pulled into a Texaco gas station while the co-worker jumped out of the truck and jogged over to the public phone. I pulled up and asked Bobby what was going on. He informed me that the co-worker knew a girl in the area who put out, as it were, and was calling her to see if we could stop over for a while.

Bobby had now changed the plan twice in one night and my mind kept racing back to the day we ended up getting stabbed by The Dad Gang. Looking back, I guess something was trying to warn me but I was not paying attention.

The girl's name was Lisa, age twenty, a mellow college coed who lived only three minutes from the gas station. As we approached the door, I heard a pretty, young voice from within. *Hi, c'mon in...*

Lisa was dressed in a university sweater and jogging pants. She was nestled into the couch, looking very comfortable and cute, and I wondered why she was up this early in the morning. Had the co-worker imposed himself and woken her up?

Our conversation trailed well into the early morning hours but not all participated. The ever bubbly co-worker's attention was focused only on the television, which I thought was rather rude. Furthermore, his leg was slung over the arm of the sofa, as if he lived there, and whenever he did happen to speak it was something obligatory to our hostess like...*Hey, do you have anything to drink?...Mind if I use the john?*

We made a quick trip to the convenience store for sodas because Lisa was all out of party goods at such short notice. Back inside the apartment, the co-worker began to mix the sodas with alcohol, opening and closing all the drawers in a noisy, crashing ceremony without anyone's permission.

"You sure know your way around in there, man," I said, making another attempt to connect with him.

"Yeah, I've been here a couple times," he replied, never looking up.

After all that kitchen contempt, his drinks ended up overtly strong and sweet. I never finished mine and Lisa took only a few sips of her glass.

I began to piece it together that the co-worker and Lisa had at one time been involved. Also obvious to me was that Lisa had taken an unabashed liking to me and her flirtations were hardly subtle.

She sat next to me on the couch and asked if she could put her cold, bare feet under my legs. Then she massaged my legs with her toes and eventually directed all her attention toward only me. Despite her attentions, our visit was quite uneventful, at least for the moment.

Chapter 13

Cocktail Of Disaster

That night I made the biggest mistake of my life. I asked Lisa if I could use her bathroom.

Located in the back of her bedroom, I entered a nightmare from which I was never to escape.

On my way out of her bedroom, Lisa came inside and quickly closed the door. With her ex-boyfriend sitting just outside, the situation had now become complex.

"George, will you do me a favor?" she whispered inside her room.

"Depends on what you're asking, Lisa."

"When you guys leave, just make sure you take that guy with you, okay?" To my surprise she was referring to the co-worker.

"What? Is something wrong?"

"Well no, but if you're leaving then he

needs to go with you, okay?"

I blinked and tried to process a response. The co-worker didn't ride with me so I really couldn't tell him what to do. Maybe Lisa should be talking to Bobby. I opened the bedroom door and called for Bobby to come in.

In retrospect, this was a really stupid thing to do. All three of us were now conducting a private conference in Lisa's bedroom, further alienating the co-worker still sitting outside, who was no doubt feeling somewhat left out.

Bobby understood that it was his responsibility to get the co-worker out of Lisa's apartment. As we all filed out of her bedroom, Lisa tugged on my sleeve and whispered something in my ear.

"George, I want you to come back."

"What?" I said, stalling to formulate a response.

I knew what she wanted but the offer would probably result in the co-worker's boot up my rear end. Oh, how I wanted to share the early morning hours with Lisa. She was smart, young and pretty and yet her attention toward me was a cocktail of disaster.

Outside in the living room we asked the co-worker if he was ready to go whereupon he answered flatly, "Nope."

That stunned all of us. Bobby and I looked at each other without a planned response. In one fell swoop the co-worker helped himself to an extended stay at Lisa's apartment.

"No, you guys go ahead," he said, taking another sip of his sticky, sweet cocktail. "I'm gonna' stay here and get a cab later."

The co-worker never shifted his gaze from the television. Never the one with role model negotiating skills, Bobby simply shrugged his shoulders and walked out the door. I trotted after him but Lisa pulled at my pants again. This time she pleaded with her hands as if in prayer. I could see the responsibility of getting the co-worker out of her apartment had fallen on me.

"C'mon man, it's really late and Bobby's your ride home. What do you say we head out?"

The co-worker looked at me with a blank stare and said, "I already *told you,* I'm staying here and I'll get a cab later."

His voice had now taken on an edge. He had officially become belligerent. I knew it was time to speak up so my heart skipped a beat.

"Look man, all ### aside, you're not welcome to stay here. Lisa doesn't want you to stay and you have to leave with us *right now.*"

Then this look tore across the co-worker's face. He dropped his legs to the ground and stood up bolt straight. I wished then that Bobby had not left in case this guy started pelting me. Instead, he looked at Lisa and asked if this was true. She looked to the ground and confessed with great difficulty that she had classes later that morning. What frightening things had gone on between them that she couldn't even tell him this simple point.

The co-worker grabbed his jacket with a huff and finally walked out the door. On my way out, Lisa again whispered for me to come back later, this time within the co-worker's hearing. What was she trying to do, get me killed?

Quickly I motioned her back inside, doing and saying anything at this point just to get out of there.

"Make sure you bolt the door and don't open up for anyone."

I turned to face the street and saw Bobby's truck take off just as the early light of dawn lit the horizon. It would have been a beautiful, frosty morning were it not for the co-worker glaring at my face, standing uncomfortably too close.

A Cry In The Wilderness

In my neighborhood, all you need is a look to know it was too late. The damage was done. All I had to do now was try to make it home.

Chapter 14

A Really Big Headache

Bobby, the co-worker and Lisa; it was like being trapped in some bad David Lynch movie.

What I describe now is to the best of my recollection the account of my demise. With the pattern of destruction by now firmly grafted into the matrix of my life, there was no way I could see this coming?

I have played and replayed the events of that insane morning over and over in my mind in the feeble attempt to determine if there was something I could have done better, or quicker, sooner or later, to prevent it from happening. Even now, the memory of this morning freezes up my soul.

"Ready to go home?" I asked the co-worker trying to stay chipper.

He said nothing and threw himself into the

passenger seat of my car. Surprisingly, Bobby had not yet taken off and was waiting for us further down the street so we drove up alongside his truck and noticed he had dozed off.

This startled him. He accidentally stepped on the accelerator and backed his truck straight into the Honda parked behind, causing significant damage. It was almost comical. I panicked, got out of the car and started yelling at Bobby.

"What the'…look what you did to that car! Are you crazy?"

The co-worker immediately used this sudden burst of chaos as an excuse to get out of the car and start running back toward Lisa's apartment and I soon found myself shouting at both of them at the same time.

"Hey, where the ### is he going?"

I took off in a jog after the co-worker. By this time Lisa had opened up thinking I was at her door. The co-worker obstructed the door with his foot and would not allow her to close it. I tapped him on the shoulder and instinctively he jerked around and looked at me, angrier than ever.

"What're you doing back here, man? C'mon, you can't stay here, we need to leave."

Just then Bobby took off. The co-worker and I watched his truck steam away, for good this time, and both of us cussed at him, agreeing on something for a change.

I despised Bobby for dumping this troubled individual on my lap. Why should I be responsible for taking this rabid creature back to his cage?

I stood there on the curb observing the events of this cold, wintry morning. There was a certain ice in the wind lashing about my face as if this were the last semblance of a normal day I would ever know.

Somehow I pried the co-worker away from Lisa's door and we slid back into my car and buckled up. As I backed out, the co-worker gave me directions to take him home. *Take a right out of the parking lot and a left on this first street.* Less than a quarter mile down the road the co-worker started in on me.

"Is there a ### problem?" he spat.

I was occupied by the street signs and traffic lights and wasn't paying attention.

"I said, is there a ### problem with something? I mean, do you have a ### problem with me?"

This time I paid attention. "Nah man, I don't have a ### problem with you." I tried my best to stay calm, if that were possible at this point.

"Well, I think you *do* have a problem with me!"

"Say, listen man," I said, feigning a yawn. "I don't know what you mean but I'm nothin' like Bobby. I'm just trying to take you home, okay? I've got no problem with you." I manufactured another yawn but he wasn't buying any of it.

"Do you have a ### problem with me?"

He was shouting at my face now so I said ## *it* and made a u-turn back to Lisa's apartment. I gave up. He could call a cab from her place and I'd be done with both of them…but it didn't quite work out quite that way.

I couldn't think clearly with this guy shouting at my face and ended up driving around in circles. I was looking for a well-lit shopping center or a family restaurant so I could run in and call 911.

Ah yes, 911? Could you come and take our friend to the Santa Rosa Mental Hospital? I'm sure he'd get a nice employee discount.

One thing was for sure; I didn't want to be driving once he started cleaning my clock. This was my wife's car and I had to bring it back in the same condition. All my caution, however, was a day late and a dollar short. I had just shifted the car into third gear when I saw his fist come at my face.

The co-worker sucker punched me in the eye and knocked my head backward into the headrest. The blow blinded my sight in that eye so now I had only half my vision. Then, with rapid succession, he punched me with his closed fist in the right temple and under both eyes.

Now the vision in both my eyes was seriously impaired and I lost all equilibrium. Each time he struck, my right arm shot upward to fend off the blows, an exercise in futility. For some hysterical reason, I was still trying to manage the steering wheel because the car careened all over the street. Where's a good cop when you need one, eh?

The next thing I knew, the co-worker was literally on top of me pounding my face. The only way he could have managed this plum position was if I had momentarily passed out. His left forearm was crushing my trachea and I couldn't breathe. This guy meant to cut off the air supply to my lungs and was quite effective in doing so. With every blow he shouted and spat down at my face.

I will kill you...punch...*I will kill you*...punch...*I will kill you*...punch...*I will kill you*...punch...

A Cry In The Wilderness

So, do you think he was mad at me, or what? He had my head pinned down between the seat and the car door while his left leg pinned my feet very nicely under the pedals of my car. From this most disadvantageous position, I was summarily immobilized.

Man, we gotta' hand it to the co-worker on his moves. H had accomplished the most beautiful lock-down position ever seen. Someone should have captured the moment on video to be studied at police academies everywhere.

Hysterically, when I came to I was trying to talk, still trying to reason with him, which only enraged him more. One really does the most degrading things within inches of losing one's life. Don't get me wrong; I could have licked this guy all by myself. Notice, that I 'had him right where I wanted him'? I'm Puerto Rican, after all.

I couldn't speak because a demonized man who was out way past his bedtime was crushing my trachea. I couldn't shout for help, give up or negotiate even if I wanted to. All that came out of my throat were garbled, unintelligible sounds.

In case you're wondering how long it took before I got some air, the answer is, about as long as it took you to read this scenario; but try to suck in your breath and simultaneously punch yourself in the face for added effect. I'm sure pictures of the injuries to my face are available somewhere upon request.

With him still pinning me down, I needed air very badly. I remember focusing on the streetlight above. *This is it; I'm dying. This guy's gonna' kill me.* My wife and little girl flashed before my eyes. *Sorry guys, I won't be coming home today.*

Just then, the will to live rose up within me and I remember reaching up to my throat. I grabbed the co-worker's pinky finger and managed to force his entire hand off my throat but it was too late. I had no more strength left, not even enough to think one final thought…*God forgive me for my sins.*

As soon as I addressed God, the co-worker slumped back into his seat, exhausted. Strange how the God thing works when you invoke it and strange how exhausted you can get when you're trying to kill someone.

Breathing now became a whole new burning labor, like breathing fire inward. I bent forward, brought my hands up to my face and that's when I noticed all the blood, blood everywhere. It was all over my hands, running down my face, dripping onto my shirt and pants. So much blood I could taste it in my mouth, plus I had a really big headache.

I looked about trying to get my bearings, trying to see through bludgeoned eyes. My larynx felt as if it were twisted into a burning knot. After about a minute or so, I began to gain full consciousness and realized what had happened. Now, I heard a noise behind me and automatically looked into the rearview mirror.

The co-worker had, at one point or another, gotten out and was now pacing back and forth at the rear of my car like a wolf man, arguing out loud with his resident demons. Now was my opportunity to burn rubber and escape. I reached for the ignition but there were no keys.

It seemed that the co-worker, ever the savvy perp' who thought of everything, had confiscated my car keys. And now he was pacing outside the car thinking of ways to show me more love.

During the co-worker's assault upon my person, I had somehow hit the brakes, caused the car to stall in third gear, leaving the engine still humming. *Maybe the car will drive without the keys?* The co-worker must have seen me fumbling around with the gear stick so he began to shout and pound his fist on the rear of my car. *Hey, hey, hey!*

I took this to mean that I better behave myself and not try any monkey business. He now paced back and forth, trying to think of what to do next.

How do I get the body out of the car? What if the cops spray Luminal? Where did I put that shovel?

Just then, it seems he had come up with a plan.

Chapter 15

Enter
The Butterfly

"**G**et out of the car! Get the ### out of the car!"

The co-worker now made his way to the front of the car and began slapping his hand on the hood.

Oh boy, he wants to finish me off. Drenched in blood, with labored breath, impaired vision and a bludgeoned face, I opened my car door in an effort to escape on foot as quickly as I could but the seat belt halted my movements. Blindly I fumbled for the buckle while keeping one eye on the co-worker. That's when my hand happened upon the compact, leather package fastened to my belt.

It was the butterfly…my lovely, stainless steel butterfly knife. Suddenly, I felt as though I might actually survive this. I blinked for a moment. *Is it true?*

Yes, there it was; my personal bodyguard of sorts, strapped to my belt. *Looks as though I'll be going home after all.*

And now, with the butterfly in hand, I took a surprisingly stronger step out of the car. By the time both my feet hit the ground, I had the knife locked and cocked at the co-worker.

He saw my knife all right, contemplated the gleaming, silver blade in my outstretched hand. He took two steps backward and began to blink his eyes rapidly. I held up the knife with ostentatious display. It glistened with deadly celebrity in the early morning light, its message perfectly clear. The co-worker would be forced to stay away from me now so I told him to relax and calm down.

I demanded the car keys so that I could leave but all he said was ### *you!* Even now, he clenched a fist and lunged forward as if to punch me. Mind-boggling. What was he on?

This time, instead of contemplating rationale, I reacted; action upon reaction, supply and demand, give and take, ying and yang.

I stepped forward and nicked him in the stomach, having no further desire to nick him again, and with a nick like that, I didn't think I'd have to.

You might be wondering why I didn't take off on foot with knife in hand. Well, I didn't think I could make it due to the burning in my lungs and throat. I stood a better chance of negotiating the keys from the co-worker's hand especially after he saw my really big knife, than negotiating the half-mile hobble to the nearest open shop. Furthermore, back in 1996 not everyone had a mobile phone. Let's see what he will do next now that I gave him the odd, quick jab in the gut.

The co-worker gawked at me. He gawked at me and then he gawked at his bleeding stomach. That's what bad guys do when they take a hit. They gawk. They can't believe they're not invincible. He looked at his stomach in disbelief, which gave me another opportunity to reason with him…*Look, man, I've got a knife. Let's not do this, okay? Just give me the ### keys so I can get the ### home.*

There should be no reason as to why anyone in their right mind would not hand over the car keys at this point, but then, the co-worker was not in his right mind. Once he saw the blood on his hand he became even more crazed, if that were possible, and again shouted vulgarities; it was comical.

Then he dove at me. This time, instead of a

nick, I stabbed him square in the chest.

I don't know how he could possibly have managed this but the co-worker put a Jujitsu move on me, kicked my legs out and sent me crashing to the payment flat on my chin.

Hey, wait a minute! I'm the one with the knife! I thought I was the bad motha' here.

His skill in martial arts surprised me. My chin hit the payment hard enough that when I looked up, he saw the fierce pain and white-hot, uncensored rage etched across on my face. Enough was enough.

I guess the knife didn't cut it for him, no pun intended, but when he saw the contortion on my face he suddenly turned and ran away.

What? Hey, if all I had to do was pull a scary face I would have done that long ago!

I don't know why but I ran after him then. Perhaps the blows to the head had crazed me. Perhaps it was the principle of the thing. In any event, I had now run out of patience. Let him keep his pound of flesh but he should at least pay me the courtesy of returning my keys. Enough was enough.

With my lungs burning, trachea bruised and eyes bludgeoned shut, I ran after him. The co-worker took off running across the street into the atrium of an apartment complex with me right behind. That must have been quite a sight. He was the guy hobbling along with blood pouring out of his chest and I was the guy hobbling after him with blood pouring out of his head.

Once inside the atrium, the co-worker stopped abruptly and spun around, realizing it presented a dead end. He just stood there staring at the blood all over me. Once again I took the defensive, butterfly in one hand and the other outstretched. With an uncomfortable silence between us, I couldn't tell what he was thinking.

Then, my mind started to play tricks on me. I began to hear him shouting again, shouting his mantra, his poem of death...*I will kill you ...I will kill you...I will kill you...*

As soon as I shook his ghostly poem out of my mind, he lunged forward and that's when it happened. I became completely lit up.

The co-worker lay there bleeding, coiled up in the fetal position with me looking over him, breathless, for what seemed to be minutes.

That's okay, he'll come around, he's got demons; they'll wake him up in a minute. I stood over him, shaking uncontrollably. *C'mon man, get up! You can kick my ass, we'll get an ambulance and call it a day!*

But he never moved again. I turned around to look out to the street. I could barely see the white fender of my car through swollen eyes and then I looked at some of the apartment doors inside the atrium: 12-C, 12-B or something.

In the early hours of February 2, 1996 I banged on doors calling for help. I couldn't shout loudly enough for anyone to hear me because my trachea was still twisted. *Hello, call 911! Hello, anybody home?*

Wasn't anybody home? So, I made my way to the next door and the one after that. *Hello, I need some help!* How could anyone have slept through all that? Come to think of it, they were probably too afraid to open the door.

The reality that I might have taken a man's life now sank in and caused me to panic. Perhaps I had become one of those evil creatures I saw when I was a kid. I went over to the co-worker and put my fingers on his neck to feel for a pulse but found none.

I staggered back to the car and collapsed into the driver's seat, contemplating the empty ignition. I just wanted to go home, take a bath and go to sleep. A few minutes later, I found the keys. He had dropped them on the concrete behind my car.

Part IV

"I was cast upon You from birth…
Be not far from me, for trouble is near
and there is none to help me."

Psalms 22:10-11

Chapter 16

The Expert

The County Coroner stated on the news the next day that a man was found dead of multiple stab wounds, nineteen to be exact, with no suspects or witnesses to the crime.

The coroner deduced that three wounds to the man's chest were fatal, one penetrating the right lung, another the left lung just below the heart and a third penetrating the heart itself.

All other wounds were superficial, non-life threatening and would have called for only routine medical attention.

That morning, instead of going home, I immediately drove in the direction of Bobby's house. And why not? With the state of mind I was in, it seemed perfectly reasonable to me at the time. Next time you get struck repeatedly about the head and face, try making executive decisions!

Where was Bobby? I wanted him to see this. It was his fault entirely and he should see the unbridled havoc he had caused. I wanted him to see how his irresponsible actions could literally alter the course of lives.

It's all your fault Bobby! You allowed this to happen to me! You left me with a drunken, belligerent psycho! You dumped your stuff on me! How come people are always dumping their stuff on me?

Wait a minute, who was I shouting at just then? As I drove to Bobby's house, the knife was still tightly clenched in my fist. I'm not too sure what time it was then but when I pulled into Bobby's driveway, he was not there!

What? Where had he been, one last merry drink while his co-worker was trying to kill me?

A few minutes later he drove up, whistling and bee-bopping into the driveway of his house. I slowly got out of my car and stood in front of him. When he saw all the blood his mouth fell open. I lunged at him, threw him against his truck and stuck my finger in his face.

"Look at me Bobby! Look at me real good!" I shouted at him. "Do you know what you did?" Bobby blinked up at me; I guess he couldn't believe what he saw. "I stabbed your friend! I stabbed him and I think he's dead!"

Bobby helped me up the steps of his house. We must have woken up his wife because she came to the front door asking questions. I quickly stepped back into the shadows of Bobby's garage while he argued her back into their bedroom. When he came back out to the garage I told him everything that had happened. He kept looking at me as though I were joking.

"Hey, do I *look like* I'm joking?"

I took off my shirt and threw it down on the concrete ground of his garage. It fell with a water-soaked thunk; only it wasn't water, it was blood, sickening, repulsive. Fear of the undead once again stole into my throat and, momentarily, I had to hold onto something. I threw all my clothes in the wash machine; long wash cycle, add five cups of Tide with bleach, safe for colors, press 'Start'.

As I walked into the early morning kitchen of Bobby's house, he handed me the phone. *Who is it? What do they want?* The voice on the other end was soothing, yet menacing.

"Now listen very carefully and you better do exactly as I tell you, got it?"

"Yeah."

It was the voice of an expert, the kind who could make people and things disappear. The man was another of Bobby's co-workers, just what I needed to whip my paranoid state of mind into an even fluffier froth. I had my fill of Bobby's co-workers but the expert was just commanding enough to arrest my attention.

The expert told me to clean the butterfly knife immediately in hot water and detergent. Then, I was to leave my clothing at Bobby's house who in turn was to destroy it. Then, I was to put on Bobby's clothing, go home and talk to no one. I would also need to clean my car of any blood evidence and get rid of the co-worker's fingerprints. Yeah right, me and what CSI lab?

"He was never in your car, got it?"

"Yeah."

"The last time you saw him was at the girl's place, got it?"

"Yeah."

"Now, go home and don't talk to anyone."

"Okay."

It was on the tip of my tongue to ask why he was such an expert on the topic of destroying evidence at crime scenes. How many of these jobs had he done, I wondered?

In the days ensuing, I tried to follow the instructions of the expert like a good boy, except the part about not talking to anyone. Now, that was hard to do.

After surviving starvation and neglect at the hands of my mother, I had actually eked out a reasonably normal life by the age of twenty-four and even served a four-year tour in the United States Coast Guard. I was by then an average, middle-class guy with a wife and kid. I was no expert in crime scene forensics nor could I have stayed quiet about any of this. Who could do that?

Let's stay home tonight. I heard the words of my Uncle Frank again and again. How was I to know it was a warning from God?

I finally stepped through the door of my grandmother's house at 7:30 A.M. on the morning of February 2, 1996. The early morning sunlight streamed in through the blinds and onto the living room carpet like the elusive, warm liquid of peace on earth. I took in the smells of my grandmother's home and the sight of all our familiar things. My Uncle Frank was sleeping on the floor with his wife and children on this golden, winter morning and I could hear my grandmother snoring peacefully in the back bedroom.

I stood there in the living room listening quietly and then I began to weep, remembering again the pleas of my Uncle Frank. *How's about you stay home tonight? We can get a couple movies, a bag of weed and some beer. Guys' night in, what dya' say?*

And then, stupidly, I answered him out loud. *It's too late for that, Frank. I'm sorry bro', Jesus, I'm so sorry.*

Not more than a couple hours earlier, I was a normal guy about to reconcile with his wife and kid and now I'm a fugitive.

Uncle Frank woke up then. I guess he must have heard what I said. He got up and followed me into the bathroom whereupon he saw my face in the light.

"George, what *happened* to you? Are you okay?"

"No Frank, I'm not okay. I think I killed a man. I stabbed him Frank and I think he's dead!"

Then, at last, I broke down and sobbed uncontrollably. Frank came close and hugged me, tried to comfort me as best as he could.

"Go to bed now George, go to sleep, c'mon now mijo, everything's gonna' be just fine."

And then I went to sleep. Later that day, Frank went about the business of white washing the truth before the interrogations of my grandmother and everyone else in the house and yet all of Frank's hard work could not erase the pain I felt hours later when I woke up.

A Cry In The Wilderness

Again Frank and I stood looking at my bludgeoned face in the bathroom mirror; by now both my eyes were bloodshot from broken vessels, left eye swollen completely shut, lips that looked like hamburger meat and purple clutch marks all over my throat, and don't forget the deep laceration on my chin.

I badly needed stitches but my face looked so injured, the medical staff at the E.R. would report me to the police on the spot. So, there we stood, looking at my face in the mirror. Good old Uncle Frank always had a joke just when you might need one.

"Damn George, what am I gonna' do with you, homes? When you do somethin'…you do it all the way, huh?"

Chapter 17

The Jelly Donuts Of My Life

My wife's sister-in-law was studying to be a lawyer. She invited us over to her house, just like Perry Mason used to do, whereupon she also told me not to tell anyone, not even the police.

Incidentally, I'd like to know what law book gives that instruction. In my heart I knew this was the wrong thing to do because I didn't kill anyone in cold blood. It was self-defense, which later turned to fear for life and then momentary insanity, perhaps due to hallucinations.

There were moments when I believed I had done the right thing. Things might have escalated. My family would have had to go after his family, then neighborhood against neighborhood; soon it would have sparked a gang war spanning over fifty years. No, this was not the kind of legacy I wanted my little girl to grow up with. If you're fat, happy, white and twenty-one, you will never understand how things work in the barrio; so don't even try.

By February 4th my grandmother found herself fending off two police detectives at eight o'clock in the morning. They had come to inquire about the injuries to my face.

One hour later, I was given the telephone number of one Melanie Martens, Attorney at Law. I called but she was not in so I quickly sped off down the road to her office and waited for hours on end until she returned, as if to seek asylum.

Once she came in, I told her the entire story. She said she would call the detectives herself, instructed me not to say one word and encouraged me not to worry about anything.

Funny, how lawyers always spoke about the mutilations of one's life as if to casually pass around donuts, the mutilated, jelly donuts of one's life. *Here, try the jelly ones; those are really good.* She told me to have pictures taken of my face and throat for the record. *I prefer the ones with chocolate sprinkles.*

She told me to go to work, go to church and "act normal" like everyone else. *On occasion, I like 'em glazed.*

Although my face was severely bludgeoned, she instructed me to return to my job at the airport and act as though nothing had happened. *Here, have another donut.*

I thought all this was hysterical, reckless advice considering the injuries to my face.

Since there were no witnesses, she said I was innocent and, therefore, none of this had ever happened. She did say, however, that my self-defense plea was "out the window" because I had left the scene of the crime.

Then, Melanie Martins gave me one final perfunctory donut. *Oh and by the way, the cops are now lookin' at you for murder one.*

On February 8th I was arrested at the airport, my place of work, for the murder of the co-worker.

"Is your name Joseph Christopher Garcia?"

A police detective suddenly stood in front of me, referring to me by my legal name, while another turned off the conveyor belt.

"Yes sir."

"Take two steps back, turn around and put your hands on that cart."

Well, I guess this is how it goes down, I

thought to myself, *so don't try anything stupid.*

As if deputy dawg heard what I was thinking, he said, "Don't try anything stupid. You're surrounded so do as I tell you."

And then, just for good measure, deputy dawg said, "Make one wrong move and I won't hesitate to shoot you."

I looked up and saw at least ten more cops all over the place, some on top of buggies, others crouching behind piles of luggage, weapons drawn and pointed at me.

Gee, if I get ten cops, how many would a guy like the co-worker get?

Gorvel Naham, Esquire, was the 'public offender' assigned to my case. I tried to explain to him that the co-worker beat the hell out of my face and that my plea should be self-defense and fear for life, or something.

"Here, Mr. Naham, take a look at the photos of my face!"

Gorv' turned out to be a useless sluggard. I could tell that this soft, wimpy guy never took a beating in his life so what could possibly have motivated him to fight for my life?

As I offered him the mutilated jelly donuts of my life, Gorv' told me to hurry up.

"Hurry up Joseph, you're too longwinded."

I protested that this was my life he was

talking about whereupon he said, "Well, what do you expect Joseph? I only get paid five hundred dollars for this job."

Then he hurried off down the jailhouse corridor and I called out after him, "But what's gonna' happen to me?"

He turned around and said, "Well, what do you think, Joseph? You *killed* a man!"

That's when I knew was in big trouble.

Chapter 18

Carnie Girl

As I sat in jail awaiting trial for the alleged murder of the co-worker, my thoughts swirled over the landscape of my mind, landing me upon the year 1987.

I was fifteen then and I suppose it was a happy year. After being rescued from the streets of New York City by county caseworkers, I was returned to San Antonio and promptly placed back into the Texas children's welfare system.

Darden Hill Ranch School, Burke Home and M.H.M.R. hosted my existence for the remainder of my teen years, whereupon I thoroughly exhausted the personnel of all three facilities. By then, an addiction to illegal narcotics, propensity toward deep depression and persistent displays of combative behavior had become permanent fixtures in my daily demeanor, deploying all available personnel around the clock. Hey, someone had to pay for the indignations of my life and it might as well have been them.

Although my dysfunctions had manifested several times throughout those years, there were many moments, which would truly touch me forever. Take for instance Elizabeth Valencia, my caseworker; she was cool and quite attractive. I sat in Elizabeth's office one day and noticed all the photos of the kids in her charge, which she had taped all over her wall; and some were photos of me!

During all those years in the system, no one in my family, not even my mother, ever wrote me a single letter nor ever came to visit me. Many times I thought, so this is what it's like to be dead, invisible.

Then, I saw those pictures of me up on Elizabeth's wall and suddenly it seemed like someone actually gave a damn. This brought a sort of healing to my young, ailing soul and propelled me, perhaps, to become a better person over the next decade.

The Helotos Festival County Fair came to town annually near the M.H.M.R. Group Home, my fourth facility to date, which turned out to be another rare set of happy days in my jagged collage of memories.

Helotos, Texas, has celebrated this county fair for decades and still does to this day. The administrators of M.H.M.R. decided we should partake in the festivities that year in order to raise money for our upcoming fishing trip by setting up a retail snack booth.

I found that working the booth channeled my teenage angst toward more constructive ground, and it just so happened, I worked that booth like an old carnie. That was where I first saw my wife… and systematically thought nothing of her.

When the days of the Helotos Festival finally arrived, the other guys noticed her down the way as we were setting up our booth and they kept inciting me to flirt with her.

"Hey George, see that girl over there?"

"Yeah, so?"

"Man, do you think she's pretty, or what?"

"No, I don't know, who cares?"

"Let's go talk to her!"

I guessed that the girl was with her mother and father helping them set up a family booth of their own to the left of ours. They were going to sell Frito Pies and fruit drinks in direct competition of our beef sandwiches and chalupas.

I paid no attention to the girl other than to look her up and down a couple times. I then channeled my energies toward sales and marketing.

Hot beef sandwiches! Come an' get 'em while they're hot! Hot beef sandwiches!

Standing out in the crowd, I shouted advertisements of our product and brought in some serious business that first day of the fair.

By the second day, I had set my eyes on the carnie girl down the way. Debra was a virgin, younger than me, tall, with shoulder length hair, full lips and chubby cheeks. I was never shy around girls and had all the smooth moves but I could tell she was pure and innocent and I would have to handle her with great delicacy. Besides, the girl's father and three brothers were big guys; needless to say, I was not about to dis' her.

On this day she was chopping onions, smelly business but always a good topic for conversation.

"Excuse me but do you always cry when you work?" She smiled then and looked at me.

"Oh, I'm just upset because my brother makes me so mad sometimes!" Those were real tears? It was not the onions?

"Hey, I'll be getting off work soon. You wanna' go on some rides?"

That warm, summer night we met up with Debra's cousin and her boyfriend and were soon skipping around the county fair just like normal kids with normal lives and I remember thinking…*So this is what it's like to be normal.*

We went on rides, had photos taken of me in a big cholo hat and even hit the dance floor with an entire audience clapping and cheering me on! Who said Michael Jackson moves don't go with Country Western?

Debra and I grew very close that summer at the county fair and I didn't want it to end. I noticed that whenever I spoke to her, she looked into my eyes. Her laugh and high-pitched voice had become a lovely melody to my heart and I couldn't wait to see her every day. Was this love I was feeling? I couldn't tell.

We exchanged telephone numbers on the last day of the county fair and I watched as this very special girl and her family packed up their gear and drove off down the road in their blue, scooby-doo van.

My mind began to race then as I watched her family drive off. I wanted to have a family of my own and I hated to see her go.

Of course, that's it! She would become my family! I would fulfill my promise to my little sister, marry that girl, live in a big house, have lots of children and never be lonely again!

At that moment I decided to marry the carnie girl from down the way. Then I twirled one last time, grabbed my pants and sang…*She told me her name was Debra Jean and she caused a scene…hee…hee.*

Debra became my wife, my best friend and the only real family I ever had after the death of my sister.

After I was arrested for the alleged murder of the co-worker, my wife divorced me and I was once again alone.

As the guards let me out into the yard my thoughts turned to my mother. I will pour out for us one final, steaming cup of indignation concerning my mother and after that, let's lay her to rest.

At the age of seventeen, I ran away from the Texas children's welfare system and they never saw me again. I actually found my mother living in Georgia with her new husband-of-the-moment named Eric and gave them a call. Right away she offered to arrange another happy reunion so I went to live with them.

Shortly after I settled in, I decided to go and see a movie at the mall to give my mother and Eric some time alone. She was supposed to pick me up at five o'clock that evening. That's right, you guessed it; I waited and waited and she never came.

I called my mother's phone number and, hysterically, it was disconnected! How could I let her do this to me again!

I was too new to the area and didn't know the bus schedule to get home so I snuck into one movie theater after another to bide the time. Five o'clock turned into eight o'clock, eight turned into ten and so forth and still no sign of Sophia.

My mother and Eric showed up at one o'clock that next morning. I fell into the back seat of their car, spitting mad, and that was when I became completely unhinged and settled the account with my mother once and for all and my rage knew no bounds as I tore into her.

"I am no longer your son!" I shouted at her face from the back seat.

"All my life you chose *men* above your own children! Don't you love me? Can't you see what you're doing? Why can't you choose me *just once!"*

My mother was momentarily stunned. Eric turned around and tried to punch me, supposing he should protect his wife, as if he had the right to judge the matter. All he managed to do, however, was rip my shirt. So I shouted at him too in case he wanted some of this. I was not so little any more.

"George! Eric and I went to the hospital

today and that's why it took us so long. Eric's been diagnosed with AIDS, you know!" She said this as if I was supposed to give a damn.

"I don't give a *damn* about Eric, mother! There you go again making excuses to avoid the truth! Just answer the question! Why have you always chosen other men above me!"

"But George, he's my husband!"

"Fine! Then I am no longer your son!" I began to spit with rage then. "You make me sick! I've always been faithful to you but *not any more*!"

When we got back to their house, Eric again tried to punch me but could not, so he resorted to throwing kitchenware at me, like some silly, pathetic, housewife crying…*You never take me anywhere!* I simply ducked and paid no attention to him.

"You are not my ### mother any more and I don't want to hear from you ever again!"

I was still shouting at the top of my lungs for all the neighbors to hear. "You and Eric can die for all I care! You are *nothing* to me anymore!"

In 1994 my mother died. Earlier that year, she had come down to Texas to meet my wife and baby girl. I could see in her face that it was just a matter of time before her addictions would take her life.

A Cry In The Wilderness

I was asleep in bed with my wife when the phone rang at three-thirty in the morning. I already knew what the call was about. A family member called to let me know that my mother had died. She had made amends with me and I, like a good Puerto Rican son, forgave all her sins.

As for me, unless I meet a Savior, the prophetic course my parents had set my life upon may very well destroy me.

Chapter 19

Code 4

As I was lying there on the jail bunker still awaiting trial for the alleged murder of the co-worker, my thoughts turned again to my years in the military. Bet you didn't know that I'm a veteran. That's right, I proudly served my country in the United States Coast Guard.

After I saw my mother for the last time, I made the decision to go back to school and earn my high school diploma. Debra and I married while we were still in high school and I held down several jobs at a time to chisel out a new life for both of us.

My heart was set on a career as a federal agent with the D.E.A. That's right, you read correctly; not because of my expertise with marijuana (nice try though) but because I had a keen desire to enter law enforcement.

I learned that instead of going to college, I could join the United States Coast Guard and work with the D.E.A. indirectly, which would look good on my resume toward a career in law enforcement. I enlisted for eight years active and four years reserve duty.

On September 8, 1992, I reported to Cape May, New Jersey, for boot camp and graduated twenty-ninth of my company after six and a half weeks training. I chose my first duty section in Seattle, Washington.

I was an outstanding recruit with not one gig (demerit) on my record the entire time. Of the sixty coed recruits in our class, I was chosen along with eight others to perform in the honor guard graduation ceremony of our company.

For the first time in my life, I was truly happy. I had married a beautiful girl, had a great career, our very own roof over our heads and a steady income. I had survived my parents and was actually making a difference in the world.

We drove from San Antonio to Seattle in the old, faithful 1980 Honda hatchback my wife's dad gave to us and only the water pump blew up. We didn't have a lot but we were happy.

Debra kept a clean house and was a good wife to me. The day of my little girl's birth truly was the greatest blessing of my life. I filmed the entire birth on video as if it were my beloved sister, Arlene, re-entering the world.

To this day, my little girl is the joy of my entire life.

I walked onto the base in full dress blues that first day, feeling like a real man and stepped proudly onto the Mariposa, a 180-foot buoy tender.

In my company, as in every military outfit, was a yeoman who harbored a thing against people of color. He was your garden-variety white man who never bothered to hide his extreme prejudice against minorities, thus throughout my tour he harangued me relentlessly. I didn't sweat the small stuff but this character went too far when he ruined my entire career prospects.

On January 1, 1994, I was unexpectedly released from the Coast Guard with an honorable discharge after a rewarding but brief tour of only two years. To my distress, someone had maliciously marked my separation paperwork as "Code 4". This code meant I would never be able to enlist in any other U.S. military branch.

Upon further inquiry, I discovered that the yeoman, a known bigot, had deliberately marked my file as "Code 4". He purported me as being "unfit and difficult to manage" and yet failed to produce a single shred of evidence to support his claim; this in sharp contrast to the *outstanding* fitness report I received during my time of training.

Further, he made the same assessment against everyone of color in his charge, which has gone unnoticed all this time, perhaps deliberately, by the Coast Guard. I consider him to be a liar and a disgrace to the uniform he wears.

When my career in the Coast Guard came to an abrupt end I had to start over. I would now have to negotiate full-time work and a college course load in criminology with a wife and newborn to care for.

Because we now found ourselves with no income, bills we couldn't pay and no place to live, it seemed very unlikely that I would achieve my higher education goals any time soon.

We ended up living with my wife's parents and I took on several odd jobs while looking for real work. I was discharged during the post Gulf War Depression and, therefore, found no work in Texas month after month.

We barely had enough money for food and diapers for our little one and, for some reason, my wife's parents refused to help us. It was like being chained to a mad roller coaster that wouldn't let you off.

My thoughts often turned to that racist yeoman during those terrible times and all the other worthy people he had done this to. I had suffered many disappointments and setbacks up to that point in my life but this one kicked the breath right out of me.

Then there was that age-old question; why are some people born into privilege and some are not? Years later, someone told me that adverse events happen to all people. Some make it out unscathed but far too many never do.

The pressure of providing for my family became so great that a new brand of desperation had taken hold of me. I ended up calling an old friend for a job.

Yeah, he gave me a job, all right, selling pot.

Shortly thereafter, my wife found a pound of weed in the garage, hit the roof, took the baby and kicked me out.

A few days before we were supposed to get back together, Bobby Lugo introduced me to his friend…the co-worker.

Chapter 20

Connally Maximus

On February 3, 1998, exactly two years after the co-worker's death, I was standing in the dayroom of the John B. Connally Maximum Security Prison, in Kenedy, Texas. Looking out the window I contemplated my fifty-year prison sentence.

Inside Connally, I was faced with new monster called hopelessness. With the future now ripped from my grasp forever, I saw the long and winding road to freedom up ahead.

What we did shortly thereafter, known as *The Texas Seven*, is something I'll regret for the rest of my life. No one was supposed to get hurt. We just wanted a chance at a normal life.

I remember looking out that window over the neatly trimmed grass lawns and barbed wire fence. *Two years down, forty-eight to go.*

I could see the road leading around the

bend, the road to somewhere, anywhere just away from here. I thought about my sister Arlene, my mother, Uncle Johnny and my grandmother. They were all dead now and all I had was time to keep me company.

Just then, the picket boss called out an announcement. *Chow time, last call, chow time!*

I took one more look at the road out there and smiled, thinking back to when I was a boy at the children's shelter. *Can't run away on an empty stomach.*

I am the voice crying in the wilderness.

Part V

"The thief comes only to
steal, kill and destroy.
But I have come to bring them
abundant Life."

John 10:10

Chapter 21

Twin Tower Power

Bad parenting skills. Are they a danger to society?

Hello, my name is Selma Kerren of Orange County, California, and I'm Joseph Garcia's co-writer. Let's have a talk, shall we?

On December 13, 2000, Joseph Garcia and the other inmates, known as *The Texas Seven*, broke out of the Connally Maximum Security Prison located sixty-two miles southeast of San Antonio. Along their escape route, they shot and killed Police Officer Aubrey Hawkins.

The subject of this book, Joseph Garcia, known to the Texas Department of Justice as Joseph Christopher Garcia, and the other escapees are now on death row at the Polunsky Unit, near Livingston, Texas, for their involvement in the death of the police officer.

Joseph Garcia

If Joseph Garcia had *half* the mother Officer Hawkins had, this conversation would not be taking place; a thought which might have repulsed the late officer's mother, yet is nevertheless true.

In January of 2007 it was announced by the Dallas media that Mrs. Jayne Hawkins, the officer's mother, succumbed to her battle with leukemia and passed away. May she rest in peace and be reunited with her beloved son.

What shall we say to a young man like Joseph Garcia? Don't worry, be happy? Things happen for a reason? Call the doctor, want some coke, have some weed? There's always a silver lining? Cheer up, it'll all work out?

Pert soliloquies seem terribly wanting at this juncture of Joseph's life and for the Hawkins' family. Fact of the matter is, Joseph's life is over now and so is Officer Hawkins'.

All his life, Joseph put his nose to the treadmill and tried to do the right thing. *Straighten up and fly right. Get a haircut and a job.* Yet nothing he ever did would succeed.

There seems to be a sort of witchcraft at work against Joseph and so many like him. Notice that his murder trial in the case of the co-worker commenced right on his birthday.

When you work with death row inmates

long enough, eventually you hear them say the same thing: "You wouldn't believe the things that happened, to put me on death row." By this they mean, of course, since the time they were born.

Shortly after the murder of her son, the mother of the slain officer accused the Texas prison system of being "so hard on inmates, it turns them into desperados."

Although we truly appreciate Mrs. Hawkins' assessment, it is not entirely accurate. There is something far more sinister at work here, specifically, the appalling negligence of far too many parents who seem to groom their children for death row early on.

Negligent parents many times set appointments for disaster years ahead of time, a fact which should be vigorously brought to their attention from the time they first bring children into this world.

Does Joseph Garcia blame his parents for the outcome of his life? No, but the co-writer of this book does.

How should society reconcile that age-old question for people like Joseph Garcia? Why are some people born into privilege and others not? Does God assign heartbreak to some and happiness to others? Hardly.

Such designations commence strictly in the home and are not dispatched from Heaven.

Setting a person on the right path in life does not take a village. It only takes one good parent, but if said parent refuses their responsibility, thank God for the village.

Joseph Garcia was born into the abject concentration camp of his parent's design and was spoon-fed regular doses of freshly squeezed misery from the time he was born. Although his is but a mild case compared to what so many children suffer at the hands of their parents in this nation, Joseph's particular brand of misery had a way of quietly spinning its insidious web in the early stages of life and corrupted every good thing that ever came his way.

This pattern, which followed him into adulthood, was so formidable, only Christ could have broken it, but for people like Joseph Garcia it is many times too late.

Many of us have been dealt a gentler hand in life, with ample opportunity to learn the social pleasantries fit for polite society. We have harnessed the basic survival skills needed to get along in this life. At the end of the day, whatever we learn in the home prevails.

Whether lawbreakers should be locked up is

not in question here. One's parenting skills are. Many will now argue that lots of people who grew up with hardships went on to become doctors and lawyers; this is true. Not all parents who have made serious mistakes are to blame and it is also true that not all children react the same way.

Today, children play out their distress more overtly than ever before as evidenced by countless schoolroom shootings, matricide and patricide. Some develop life-long behavioral disorders while others kick it up a notch and turn to serial crime for relief. Just ask the FBI.

Attempting to lump all children into the same 'doctor-lawyer mold' could render us ill prepared for consequence. In other words, poke a stick at a dog long enough, he'll turn around and bite you.

The truth is all kids do not come from the same assembly line. Some compose great symphonies and others build rockets. Some defend our nation while others design machinery or discover medical breakthroughs. Some are prone to passion and others to lethargy, some are combustive and others passive.

To demand the same outcome of every child-at-risk is absurd and nothing more than a game of chance; roll the dice and take your chances. Throw your kid away and we might all live to regret it.

Joseph Garcia, like so many other inmates, was pushed to the limit once too often and never learned the necessary coping skills to get along in this life, not for long anyway.

It is a well-known fact among state and county caseworkers that lower income families are the breeding ground for early childhood developmental breakdowns.

Just when the lower-income family scrapes together a little money, the car breaks down. Now, they have no way to work, which threatens their income. That next month they can finally pay the rent but dad gets laid off at the plant. A single mom blows a flat tire on the freeway? Now she must choose between groceries and a tow truck.

To us these are simply the ordinary motions of everyday life, the garden-variety ups and downs but to the family at-risk, such events quickly take on monumental proportions.

Poverty is an equal opportunity destroyer. One unexpected problem can mean the difference between a roof over their heads one day and homelessness the next. For many families the trick is to ascend from poverty and stay out.

Now, imagine such hardships coming down full force upon two lone children, one an invalid, who are left to fend for themselves day after day, and on city streets, no less.

Joseph Garcia was thrown away by his parents on several levels: food, clothing, shelter, education, self-esteem, medical attention, safety and protection. As a result of this neglect, when faced with distress later in life, his mind snapped.

Adults of his background are simply not wired correctly and can only react in the way they have been taught.

In an unparalleled display of bad taste, then Dallas prosecutor Toby Shook, stuck a finger at Joseph Garcia's face during closing arguments and, shouting all the way, mocked him in open court about his bio-father throwing him away, and that his step-father had done the same, thereby daring to imply that Joseph, the child, was evil and deserved it.

Having used this hideous courtroom tactic, the prosecutor systematically slaps all abused children across the face and deems them worthless, while reducing his office to a useless lump of lard. Shook was recently elected as the new Dallas District Attorney.

The case against wicked parents thickens.

Take for example Lyle and Erik Menendez, now serving life sentences in separate California prisons for the 1989 shotgun murders of their parents. During the much-publicized trial, the brothers told of episodes wherein their father stuck thumbtacks into their buttocks and thighs, after which he bent them over a dresser and, well, you fill in the blanks.

There was no reason to doubt the allegations since several family members testified that the father spent way too much time with the boys inside their bedrooms.

After years of such abuse why did society expect the Menendez boys to have the wherewithal to show constraint later in life?

And then we have Charles Manson, our favorite poster child of crime. Despite the fact that we love to hate him, Manson also didn't just grow on a tree. He suffered untold abuse at the hands of his crazed, prostitute mother from the moment he was born to the day he ran away from home. From the age of five she forced him to watch on as she engaged in sex acts with multiple johns and eventually forced the tiny, thin boy to join in.

Then, just for being in the way, she regularly beat him within an inch of his life and locked him up outside in a tool shed for days on end in the middle of an Appalachian winter. The child that emerged from the tool shed was a monster.

In March of 2006, a seventeen-year old boy by the name of Cody Posey, was found guilty of fatally shooting his father, stepmother and teenage half-sister at a New Mexico ranch, owned by über-journalist Sam Donaldson.

During the televised trial, countless witnesses came forward testifying that the boy's father severely beat and humiliated Cody Posey from the time he was an infant up to the time of the killings. A ranch-hand testified he intervened in one such beating while the boy was yet in diapers. On this particular occasion, said the ranch-hand, the beating was so severe the toddler was found "gasping for air".

The abuse against Cody Posey was so great that the father of the teenage girl, whom Cody had killed, stepped forward and told the judge he would gladly take the boy into his own house even though he had just killed his daughter.

None of these witnesses ever once alerted authorities as to the terrors the boy suffered day after day. As a teen, Cody Posey tried to get help from school counselors who also did nothing to help him.

The reason given by Cody Posey for killing his entire family was that toward the end his father had demanded he engage in sex acts with his stepmother, which they planned on photographing and posting on an 'incest website'. The boy snapped, grabbed a shotgun and killed them all.

Although pornography was found on the deceased father's computer showing explicit photographs of incest-sex between fathers and daughters, mothers and sons, the prosecutor in the case rejected Posey's claim and tried to sell it to the jury that theirs was a happy, normal home.

Cody Posey received a light sentence in juvenile hall and will soon be released. Apparently, juries are becoming increasingly aware as to the torte effects of abuse.

Whether violent criminals should be locked up is not in question here; what pushes them to commit their crimes is.

Hysterically, society actually expects survivors of abuse to have the "wherewithal" to act responsibly while suffering under outrageous strains that none of us would ever tolerate; strains which, furthermore, destroy the child's *very ability* to think clearly in the first place. That's why we have counseling.

Trial after trial such expectations become an exercise in futility, like trying to squeeze logic from a turnip. Before too long it becomes perfectly clear that bad parenting skills are a danger to society. Equally alarming is that early intervention literally saves lives!

Perhaps our laws on 'contributing to the delinquency of a minor' and 'aiding and abetting' should be revisited and expanded?

God the Creator is trying to alert us to some very serious business here in the area of parenting. We hardly need Bible scripture to drive the point home. Most damning of all are the warnings of mental health professionals, that if we tell a child long enough he is worthless and will never amount to anything, that is exactly how he will end up.

Like bigotry, failure is a behavior learned in the home.

Unbeknownst to many parents, they have the power to twist and turn a child's entire life by the evil or good they "prophesy" over them, through action, word and deed.

Those who refused to care for Joseph set the evil appointments in motion, described in this book, decades earlier. Had they cared for him properly, Joseph might have experienced a happy, normal existence, gone on to become a federal agent and family man. Had they cared for him properly, Joseph might never have met the co-worker or been involved in the police officer's death, and this conversation might not be taking place.

We all watched in disbelief as the Twin Towers fell to the ground on September 11, 2001. Many preachers in America declared on worldwide television that the 9/11 attacks were "God's judgment against America".

The same preachers are video-cataloged shouting the identical things about the disaster victims of Hurricane Katrina and Tsunami, claiming they "got exactly what they deserved".

Should we be surprised? The church has been using the Name of God to scare the world for centuries, a really bad habit that has gone uncontested just as long.

Such conjecture is not only perverse but also complete nonsense, for the simple reason it does not match the true words of Christ on any level. On the contrary, it was *evil men* who exercised their free will *to do evil* on September 11th and God had nothing to do with it!

Evil men came to steal, kill and destroy, thus we have no right to implicate God in the chaos mankind creates.

Stay with us…there's a point here.

The most difficult thing for people to accept is that God cannot intervene against our free will unless someone asks Him to.

Thus, the consequence of free will when used for evil can be permanent and devastating. We have only to watch the six o'clock news to see how true this is.

Now, if free will can bring down two skyscrapers in less than an hour, think of what it can do to some little kid. Think of what it can do to someone else's kid.

The Texas Seven were desperados, in the suffering sense, long before the escape took place. The Texas Department of Corrections merely received them that way.

The appointments of disaster had been set in motion decades earlier by those who set the men on that particular path.

Just ask Randy Halprin, the youngest of the Texas Seven. Halprin was kicked out of his Kentucky Baptist home for troubled youth while still a minor for benign infractions such as 'kissing in public'. With no place else to go he ended up destitute at a homeless shelter and, still traumatized, got himself into considerable trouble. Had his Christian counselors continued to work with him, which was their job to do,

Randy Halprin would have stood a chance. Instead, he found himself headed for death row only two years later.

At the end of the day, Joseph Garcia got the chance to make amends with his mother. It was not he who needed amendment; she did. His mother and many of his relatives are now dead. Joseph is on death row and his two fathers have gotten away with it, free as larks.

The day of reckoning is coming, however, for all such appointment-setters. Take a look at the words of Christ in Matthew 18:6:

> "If anyone breaks one of these little children, it would be better for him that a millstone turned by an ass be hung around his neck and he be sunk into the depth of the sea."

This particular version is the original Greek, delightfully more gruesome than the quaint, English rendition. As you can tell, Christ minced no words concerning the topic of people who break down kids and turn them into beings of regret.

Clearly, Judgment Day will come as a welcome relief to many.

Please think about how you are raising your

children. Are you grooming them to do good or evil, to make a difference or to rob other parents of their children? Are you setting appointments for future disasters?

It's not too late to cancel them. If the situation in your home is out of control, please seek help from counselors and programs in your local community, and don't be ashamed to ask.

And if you are so inclined, ask Christ to help you. Find a happy, strong church to attend, and flourish there. Taking positive steps will change the course of your child's life forever. Break the cycle and make the change. You'll be applauded for doing the right thing, in this world and the next.

This story written by George aka Joseph Garcia does not exploit his membership in the notorious Texas Seven prison gang nor does it rail against the Texas prison system. He is merely confessing his own sins and exposing the sins committed against his person from the time he was born.

Joseph wants to leave something of himself behind for his teenage daughter, Arlene, something that might speak to someone, somewhere.

Many will hotly disagree that a parent

determines one's destiny and yet everyone agrees that far too many kids are thrown away every day. We also agree that under-privileged children continue to stare us squarely in the face. On what point then, do we disagree?

If one of these kids ever asks you why terrible things happened to them, you won't know how to answer but you can help them with immediate intervention.

Maybe you will try to offer them the sorry, worn-out adage that 'all things happen for a reason'. Just because something sounds poetic doesn't make it true. Christ said evil comes *only* to steal, kill and destroy, and that means there is no fruit or reason in any of it, ever.

Sadly, conjecture of any sort is a day late and a dollar short for the mother, wife and son of Police Officer Aubrey Hawkins.

There's only one message in this book: Parents, take care of your kids before they hurt someone.

Some things should never have happened and this conversation should not be taking place.

Selma Kerren
Orange County
California

The Lord forgives all your sins
He heals all your diseases
He rescues your life from destruction
He crowns you with loving kindness
And tender mercies
He satisfies your mouth with good things
So that your youth is restored like the eagle's
The Lord executes righteousness and justice
For all who are oppressed
For as the heavens are high above the earth
So great is His mercy toward all who fear Him
As a father pities His children
So the Lord pities those who fear Him
For He knows our frailty
He remembers that we are dust.

Psalms 103:1-6

If you would like to correspond with
Joseph Garcia, please write:

Joseph Christopher Garcia
#999441
Polunsky Unit D/R
3872, FM 350 South
Livingston, TX 77351
USA

If you would like to correspond with
Selma Kerren, please write:

skerren@hotmail.com

Look for other books by Selma Kerren
Soon to be released at book retailers everywhere:

Did God Really Say That?
The Answer Is No!
Matching old-church rhetoric
Against the true words of Christ.

And

Destiny
A story of tribulation and triumph
Set in the 1890's Deep South.